"Amidst a contemporary Christian culture characterized by rampant confusion regarding the central tenets of our faith, Greg Gilbert has given us a portrait of the gospel that is clear for those who have believed and compelling for those who have yet to believe. Word-saturated, cross-centered, and God-exalting, *What Is the Gospel?* will capture your mind's attention and ignite your heart's affection for the God who saves us by his grace through his gospel for his glory."

—DAVID PLATT, Pastor-Teacher,
McLean Bible Church

"Clarity on the gospel brings both confidence in the gospel and conviction concerning core gospel truths. This excellent book is wonderfully clear and biblically faithful, and will repay reading with renewed gospel focus."

—WILLIAM TAYLOR, Rector,
St. Helen Bishopsgate, London

"When I think of the centerpiece of my Bible, my heart immediately embraces the gospel. I know many people who love the gospel, but I'm always open to loving it more and understanding it better. Greg Gilbert has written this book to help us to know and love the gospel more."

—JOHNNY HUNT, Senior Vice President of Evangelism
and Leadership, North American Mission Board

"What makes this book profound is its simplicity. Perhaps the greatest danger in Christianity is making assumptions about what the gospel is without hearing the Bible's clear and definitive voice. It is not an overstatement to say this may be the most important book you'll read about the Christian faith."

—RICK HOLLAND, Senior Pastor,
Mission Road Bible Church,
Prairie Village, Kansas

What Is the
Gos•pel?

Greg Gilbert
Foreword by D. A. Carson

::: CROSSWAY®

WHEATON, ILLINOIS

What Is the Gospel?
Copyright © 2010 by Gregory D. Gilbert
Published by Crossway
          1300 Crescent Street
          Wheaton, Illinois 60187

Cover design: Dual Identity Design

First printing 2010

Printed in the United States of America

Hardcover ISBN: 978-1-4335-1500-2
PDF ISBN: 978-1-4335-1501-9
Mobipocket ISBN: 978-1-4335-1502-6
ePub ISBN: 978-1-4335-2460-8

Library of Congress Cataloging-in-Publication Data
Gilbert, Greg, 1977–
   What is the Gospel? / Greg Gilbert ; foreword by D. A.
Carson.
      p.   cm.
   Includes bibliographical references and index.
   ISBN 978-1-4335-1500-2 (hc)
   1. Theology, Doctrinal—Popular works. I. Title.
BT77.G44   2010
230—dc22   2009030583

Crossway is a publishing ministry of Good News Publishers.

LB		31	30	29	28	27	26	25	24	23	22	
33	32	31	30	29	28	27	26	25	24	23	22	21

To Moriah

I love you.

Tons and tons.

Contents

Series Preface

The 9Marks series of books is premised on two basic ideas. First, the local church is far more important to the Christian life than many Christians today perhaps realize. We at 9Marks believe that a healthy Christian is a healthy church member.

Second, local churches grow in life and vitality as they organize their lives around God's Word. God speaks. Churches should listen and follow. It's that simple. When a church listens and follows, it begins to look like the One it is following. It reflects his love and holiness. It displays his glory. A church will look like him as it listens to him.

By this token, the reader might notice that all "9 marks," taken from Mark Dever's 2001 book, *Nine Marks of a Healthy Church* (Crossway Books), begin with the Bible:

- expositional preaching;
- biblical theology;
- a biblical understanding of the gospel;
- a biblical understanding of conversion;
- a biblical understanding of evangelism;
- a biblical understanding of church membership;
- a biblical understanding of church discipline;
- a biblical understanding of discipleship and growth; and
- a biblical understanding of church leadership.

More can be said about what churches should do in order to be healthy, such as pray. But these nine practices are the ones that we believe are most often overlooked today (unlike prayer). So our basic message to churches is, don't look to the best business practices or the latest styles; look to God. Start by listening to God's Word again.

Out of this overall project comes the 9Marks series of books. These volumes intend to examine the nine marks more closely and from different angles. Some target pastors. Some target church members. Hopefully all will combine careful biblical examination, theological reflection, cultural consideration, corporate application, and even a bit of individual exhortation. The best Christian books are always both theological and practical.

It's our prayer that God will use this volume and the others to help prepare his bride, the church, with radiance and splendor for the day of his coming.

Foreword

More than thirty years of teaching theological students have shown me that the most controverted questions they ask vary from generation to generation—and the same is true of the broader Christian public. At one time you could guarantee a heated debate by throwing out the question, What do you think of the charismatic movement? or Is inerrancy worth defending? or What do you think about seeker-sensitive churches? It is easy enough to find people willing to discuss these questions today, but there is usually little heat left in them and not much more light. Today the question most likely to light a fuse is—as the author of this volume points out— What is the gospel? One might usefully add that question's first cousin, What is evangelicalism?

That these questions engender mutually exclusive answers, often dogmatically defended with only a minimum of reflection on the Bible, is, quite frankly, alarming, because the issues are so fundamental. When "evangelicals" hold highly disparate opinions about what the "evangel" is (that is, the "gospel," for that is what "evangel" means), then one must conclude either that evangelicalism as a movement is a diverse phenomenon with no agreed gospel and no sense of responsibility "to contend for the faith" that the Lord has "once for all entrusted" to us, his people (Jude 3 NIV), or that many people call themselves "evangelicals" who do not have any legitimate right to do so because they have left the "evangel," the gospel, behind.

Enter Greg Gilbert. This book does not so much claim to break new ground as survey afresh some old ground that should never have been ignored, much less abandoned. The clarity of Greg's thought and articulation is wholly admirable. This book will sharpen the thinking of not a few mature Christians. More importantly, it is a book to distribute widely to church leaders, young Christians, and even some who have not yet trusted Christ who want a clear explanation of what the gospel is. Read it, then buy a box of them for generous distribution.

D. A. Carson

Introduction

What is the gospel of Jesus Christ?

You'd think that would be an easy question to answer, especially for Christians. In fact, you'd think that writing a book like this—one asking Christians to think carefully about the question, What is the gospel of Jesus?—would be completely unnecessary. It's like asking carpenters to sit around and ponder the question, What is a hammer?

After all, the gospel of Jesus Christ stands at the very center of Christianity, and we Christians claim to be about the gospel above all else. It's what we intend to found our lives upon and build our churches around. It's what we speak to others about, and it's what we pray they also will hear and believe.

For all that, how firm a grasp do you think most Christians really have on the content of the Christian gospel? How would you answer if someone asked you: What is this news that you Christians go on and on about? And what's so good about it?

My sense is that far too many Christians would answer with something far short of what the Bible holds out as "the gospel of Jesus Christ." Maybe they'd answer, "The gospel is that God will forgive your sins if you believe in him." Or they'd say something like, "The good news is that God loves you and has a wonderful plan for your life." Or, "The gospel is that you are a child of God, and God wants his children to be abundantly successful in every way." Some would know that it's important to say something about Jesus' death on the cross and his resurrection, but then again, how does all that fit in?

The fact is, getting Christians to agree on an answer to the question, What is the gospel? is not as simple as it should be. I work with a ministry called 9Marks, an organization affiliated with Capitol Hill Baptist Church in Washington DC. For the most part, those who read and comment on our material are from a pretty narrow slice of evangelical Christianity. They believe the Bible is true and inerrant, they believe Jesus died on the cross and rose bodily from the dead, they believe human beings are sinners in need of salvation, and they intend to be gospel-centered, gospel-saturated people.

But what would you guess is the topic that single-handedly generates the most comment and the most energetic response of anything we write on? Yep, it's the gospel. We can write and speak for months about preaching, discipling, counseling, church polity, even church music, and the response from our readers is interesting but not surprising. But let us post an article trying to be clear about what the Bible teaches is the good news of Christianity, and the response is stunning.

Some time ago, one of my friends posted a short article on our website about a well-known Christian artist who had been asked in an interview to define what the good news of Christianity is. Here's what the artist said:

> What a great question. I guess I'd probably . . . my instinct is to say that it's Jesus coming, living, dying, and being resurrected

and his inaugurating the already and the not yet of all things being restored to himself . . . and that happening by way of himself . . . the being made right of all things . . . that process both beginning and being a reality in the lives and hearts of believers and yet a day coming when it will be more fully realized. But the good news, the gospel, the speaking of the good news, I would say is the news of his kingdom coming, the inaugurating of his kingdom coming . . . that's my instinct.

Several of us responded by asking questions such as, "If we're articulating the Christian gospel, shouldn't we include some *explanation* of Jesus' death and resurrection?" Or, "Shouldn't we say something about sin and the need for salvation from God's wrath against it?"

The response to that series of posts was incredible. For literally months, we received dozens of messages about it. Some who wrote to us appreciated the questions we raised; others wondered what was wrong with articulating the gospel like that since Jesus preached about the arrival of the kingdom. Others were just refreshed to hear Christians thinking hard about how to articulate the gospel in the first place.

In some ways, I'm glad to see Christians getting excited when a discussion about the gospel begins. It means they're taking it seriously, and that they have deeply held thoughts about what the gospel is. There would be nothing healthy at all in Christians who couldn't care less how we define and understand the gospel. On the other hand, I think the energy generated by discussions about the gospel points to a general fog of confusion that swirls around it these days. When you come right down to it, Christians just don't agree on what the gospel is—even Christians who call themselves evangelical.

Ask any hundred self-professed evangelical Christians what the good news of Jesus is, and you're likely to get about sixty different answers. Listen to evangelical preaching, read evangelical books, log on to evangelical websites, and you'll find one description after another of the gospel, many of them mutually exclusive. Here are a few I've found:

> The good news is, God wants to show you his incredible favor. He wants to fill your life with "new wine," but are you willing to get rid of your old wineskins? Will you start thinking bigger? Will you enlarge your vision and get rid of those old negative mind-sets that hold you back?

> Here's the gospel in a phrase. Because Christ died for us, those who trust in him may know that their guilt has been pardoned once and for all. What will we have to say before the bar of God's judgment? Only one thing. Christ died in my place. That's the gospel.

> The message of Jesus may well be called the most revolutionary of all time: "The radical revolutionary empire of God is here, advancing by reconciliation and peace, expanding by faith, hope, and love—beginning with the poorest, the weakest, the meekest, and the least. It's time to change your thinking. Everything is about to change. It's time for a new way of life. Believe me. Follow me. Believe this good news so you can learn to live by it and be part of the revolution."

> The good news is that God's face will always be turned toward you, regardless of what you have done, where you have been, or how many mistakes you've made. He loves you and is turned in your direction, looking for you.

The gospel itself refers to the proclamation that Jesus, the crucified and risen Messiah, is the one, true, and only Lord of the world.

Good news! God is becoming King and he is doing it through Jesus! And therefore, *phew!*, God's justice, God's peace, God's world is going to be renewed. And in the middle of that, of course, it's good news for you and me. But that's the derivative from, or the corollary of the good news which is a message about Jesus that has a second-order effect on me and you and us. But the gospel is not itself about *you are this sort of a person and this can happen to you.* That's the result of the gospel rather than the gospel itself. . . . Salvation is *the result of* the gospel, not the center of the gospel itself.

The gospel is the proclamation of Jesus, in [two] senses. It is the proclamation *announced* by Jesus—the arrival of God's realm of possibility (his "kingdom") in the midst of human structures of possibility. But it is also the proclamation *about* Jesus—the good news that in dying and rising, Jesus has made the kingdom he proclaimed available to us.

As a Christian, I am simply trying to orient myself around living a particular kind of way, the kind of way that Jesus taught is possible. And I think that the way of Jesus is the best possible way to live. . . . Over time when you purposefully try to live the way of Jesus, you start noticing something deeper going on. You begin realizing the reason this is the best way to live is that it is rooted in profound truths about how the world is. You find yourself living more and more in tune with ultimate reality. You are more and more in sync with how the universe is at its deepest levels. . . . The first Christians announced this way of Jesus as "the good news."

> My understanding of Jesus' message is that he teaches us to live in the reality of God now—here and today. It's almost as if Jesus just keeps saying, "Change your life. Live this way."

You see what I mean when I say the gospel is surrounded by a fog of confusion! If you had never heard of Christianity, what would you think after reading those few quotations? You'd obviously know that Christians intend to be communicating some message that is good. But beyond that, it's just a jumble. Is the good news simply that God loves me, and that I need to start thinking more positively? Is it that Jesus is a really good example who can teach me to live a loving and compassionate life? It might have something to do with sin and forgiveness. Apparently some Christians think this good news has something to do with Jesus' death. Others apparently don't.

My point is not to decide here and now which of these quotations are better or worse than the others (though I hope that after reading this book you'll be able to decide). It's simply to point out how many different things come to people's minds when they're asked, What is the gospel?

I want to try in this book to offer a clear answer to that question, one that is based on what the Bible itself teaches about the gospel. In the process, I am hoping and praying for several things.

First, if you are a Christian, I pray that this little book—and more importantly, the glorious truths it attempts to articulate—will cause your heart to swell with joy and praise toward Jesus Christ for what he has accomplished for you. An emaciated gospel leads to emaciated worship. It lowers our eyes from God to self and cheapens what God has accomplished for us in Christ. The biblical gospel, by contrast, is like fuel in the furnace of worship. The more you understand about it, believe it, and rely on it, the more you adore God both for who he is and for what he has done for us in Christ. "Oh, the depth of the riches and wisdom and knowledge of God!" Paul cried (Rom. 11:33), and it was because his heart was full of the gospel.

Second, I hope that reading this book will give you a deeper confidence as you talk to others about the good news of Jesus. I have met any number of Christians who hesitate to share the gospel with friends, family, and acquaintances for fear of not having answers to all their questions. Well, it's probably true, no matter who you are, that you'll never be able to answer *all* the questions! But you *can* answer *some* of them, and I hope this book will help you answer *more* of them.

Third, I pray that you will see the importance of this gospel for the life of the church, and that as a result you will work to make sure that this gospel is preached, sung, prayed, taught, proclaimed, and heard in every aspect of your church's life. It is through the church, Paul says, that the manifold wisdom of God will be made known to the universe. And how is that? Through the preaching of the gospel, which brings to light "for everyone" God's eternal plan to save the world (Eph. 3:7–12).

Fourth, I hope this book will help to shore up the edges of the gospel in your mind and heart. The gospel is a stark message, and it intrudes into the world's thinking and priorities with sharp, bracing truths. Sadly, there has always been a tendency among Christians—even among evangelicals—to soften some of those edges so that the gospel will be more readily acceptable to the world. One of my prayers is that this book will serve to preserve those edges and prevent the erosion of truths that, though hard for the world to swallow, are indispensable to the good news of Jesus. All of us are tempted, in the name of being winsome witnesses, to present the gospel in as attractive a way as possible. That's fine in some respects—it is "*good news*," after all—but we must also be careful not to round off the gospel's sharp points. We must preserve the edges, and I hope this book will help us to do that.

Finally, if you're not a Christian, then I pray that by reading this book you will be provoked to think hard about the good news of Jesus Christ. This is the message on which we Christians have staked our entire lives, and it's one that we believe demands a response from you, too. If there's anything in the world that you cannot afford to ignore, it is the voice of God saying, "Good news! Here is how you can be saved from my judgment!" That's the kind of announcement that demands attention.

1

Finding the Gospel in the Bible

Did you know that GPS navigation systems are causing havoc in towns across the United States? That's especially the case in small towns. For people who live in large cities, the little machines are lifesavers. Plug the GPS in, type in an address, and you're off to the races. No more missed exits, no more wrong turns—just you, your car, your GPS, and ding! "Arriving at destination!"

I just recently got my first GPS device, which was primarily an act of defiance against whoever is responsible for the almost impossible road system in Washington DC. My first experience with it, though, wasn't in Washington. It was in Linden, Texas, my very small, very rural, and very out-of-the-way hometown.

It turns out that my GPS has no problem whatsoever navigating the crisscrossing, back-and-forth streets of Washington. Oddly enough, though, it did have trouble in Linden. Roads that the GPS was quite certain existed, didn't. Turns that it insisted were possible, weren't. Addresses that it firmly believed would be in a certain place, turned out to be several hundred yards further down the street—or even nonexistent.

Apparently GPS systems' ignorance of small towns is a growing problem. ABC News ran a story about neighborhood roads that have literally become commercial thoroughfares because GPS systems are routing traffic there, rather than along larger highways. There are other problems, too. One poor guy from California insisted he was only following his GPS's instructions when he made a right turn onto a rural road and found himself stuck on a train track, staring into the headlight of an oncoming locomotive! He survived. His rental car, though, and presumably the offending GPS along with it, didn't make out so well.

One representative from the American Automobile Association was sympathetic—kind of. "Clearly the GPS failed him in the sense it should not have been telling him to make a right turn on the railroad tracks," he said. "But just because a machine tells you to do something that is potentially dangerous, doesn't mean you should do it." Indeed!

So what's going on? GPS manufacturers say the problem isn't with the devices themselves. They're doing exactly what they're supposed to do. Instead, the problem is in the maps the devices are downloading. It turns out that especially for small towns, the maps available to GPS systems are often several years, or even decades, out of date. Sometimes the maps are nothing better than planning maps—what city planners *intended* to do if their towns grew. The result? Sometimes addresses that show up in one place on the planning maps ended up being somewhere else when the town was actually built. Sometimes roads that city planners intended to build never actually got built—and sometimes they got built not as roads at all, but as railroads!

In the world of GPS, as in life, it's important that you get your information from a reliable source!

What's Our Authority?

The same thing is true when we approach the question, What is the gospel? Right at the beginning, we have to make some sort of decision about what source of information we're going to use in order to answer the question. For evangelicals, the answer usually comes pretty easily: we find the answer in the Bible.

That's true, but it's useful to know up front that not everyone agrees entirely with that answer. Different "Christian" traditions have given a number of different answers to this question of authority. Some have argued, for instance, that we ought to base our understanding of the gospel not solely, or even primarily, on the words of the Bible, but on Christian tradition. If the church has believed something for long enough, they argue, we should understand it to be true. Others have said that we know truth through the use of reason. Building our knowledge from the ground up—A leads to B leads to C leads to D—will bring us to a true understanding of ourselves, the world, and God. Still others say we should look for the truth of the gospel in our own experience. Whatever resonates most with our own hearts is what we finally understand to be true about ourselves and God.

If you spend enough time thinking about it, though, you realize that each of those three potential sources of authority ultimately fails to deliver what it promises. Tradition leaves us relying on nothing more than the opinions of men. Reason, as any freshman philosopher will tell you, leaves us flailing about in skepticism. (Try to *prove*, for example, that you're not just a figment of someone else's imagination, or that your five senses really are reliable.) And experience leaves us relying on our own fickle hearts in order to decide what is true—a prospect most honest people find unsettling at best.

What do we do, then? Where do we go in order to know what is true, and therefore what the good news of Jesus Christ really is? As Christians, we believe that God has spoken to us in his Word, the Bible. Furthermore, we believe that what God has said in the Bible is infallibly and inerrantly true, and therefore it leads us not to skepticism or despair or uncertainty, but to confidence. "All Scripture is breathed out by God," Paul said, "and profitable for teaching" (2 Tim. 3:16). King David wrote,

> This God—his way is perfect;
>   the word of the LORD proves true. (Ps. 18:30)

And so it is to God's Word that we look in order to find what he has said to us about his Son Jesus and about the good news of the gospel.

Where in the Bible Do We Go?

But where do we go in the Bible to find that? I suppose there are several different approaches we could take. One would be to look at all the occurrences of the word *gospel* in the New Testament and try to come to some sort of conclusion about what the writers mean when they use the word. Surely there are a few instances where the writers are careful to define it.

There could be important things to learn from this approach, but there are drawbacks, too. One is that often in the New Testament a writer obviously intends to give a summary of the good news of Christianity, yet he doesn't use the word *gospel* at all. Take Peter's sermon at Pentecost in Acts 2, for example. If ever there was a proclamation of the good news of Christianity, surely this is it—yet Peter never mentions the word *gospel*. Another example is the apostle John, who uses the word only once in all his New Testament writings (Rev. 14:6)!

Let me suggest that, for now, we approach the task of defining the main contours of the Christian gospel not by doing a word study, but by looking at what the earliest Christians said about Jesus and the significance of his life, death, and resurrection. If we look at the apostles' writings and sermons in the Bible, we'll find them explaining, sometimes very briefly and sometimes at greater length, what they learned from Jesus himself about the good news. Perhaps we'll also be able to discern some common set of questions, some shared framework of truths around which the apostles and early Christians structured their presentation of the good news of Jesus.

The Gospel in Romans 1–4

One of the best places to start looking for a basic explanation of the gospel is Paul's letter to the Romans. Perhaps more clearly than any other book of the Bible, Romans contains a deliberate, step-by-step expression of what Paul understood to be the good news.

Actually, the book of Romans is not so much a *book* at all, at least as we usually think of books. It's a letter, a way for Paul to introduce himself and his message to a group of Christians he had never met. That's why it has such a systematic, step-by-step feel. Paul wanted these Christians to know about him, his ministry, and especially his message. He wanted them to know that the good news he preached was the same good news they believed.

"I am not ashamed of the gospel," he begins, "for it is the power of God for salvation to everyone who believes" (Rom. 1:16). From there, especially through the first four chapters, Paul explains the good news about Jesus in wonderful detail. As we look at these chapters, we'll see that Paul structures his presentation of the gospel around a few critical truths, truths that show up again and again in the apostles' preaching of the gospel. Let's look at the progression of Paul's thought in Romans 1–4.

First, Paul tells his readers that it is God to whom they are accountable. After his introductory remarks in Romans 1:1–7, Paul begins his presentation of the gospel by declaring that "the wrath of God is revealed from heaven" (v. 18). With his very first words, Paul insists that humanity is not autonomous. We did not create ourselves, and we are neither self-reliant nor self-accountable. No, it is God who created the world and everything in it, including us. Because he created us, God has the right to demand that we worship him. Look what Paul says in verse 21: "For although they knew God, they did not honor him as God or give thanks to him, but they became futile in their thinking, and their foolish hearts were darkened."

Thus Paul indicts humanity: they have sinned by not honoring and thanking God. It is our obligation, as people created and owned by God, to give him the honor and glory that is due to him, to live and speak and act and think in a way that recognizes and acknowledges his authority over us. We are made by him, owned by him, dependent on him, and therefore accountable to him. That's the first point Paul labors to make as he explains the good news of Christianity.

Second, Paul tells his readers that their problem is that they rebelled against God. They—along with everyone else—did not honor God and give thanks to him as they should have. Their foolish hearts were darkened and they "exchanged the glory of the immortal God for images resembling mortal man and birds and animals and creeping things" (v. 23). That's a truly revolting image, isn't it? For human beings to consider their Creator and then decide that a wooden or metal image of a frog or a bird or even *themselves* is more glorious, more satisfying, and more valuable is the height of insult and rebellion against God. It is the root and essence of sin, and its results are nothing short of horrific.

For most of the next three chapters Paul presses this point, indicting all humanity as sinners against God. In chapter 1 his focus is on the Gentiles, and then in chapter 2 he turns just as strongly toward the Jews. It's as if Paul knows that the most self-righteous of the Jews would have been applauding his lashing of the Gentiles, so he pivots on a dime in 2:1 and points his accusing finger at the applauders: "Therefore *you* have no excuse"! Just like Gentiles, he says, Jews have broken God's law and are under his judgment.

By the middle of chapter 3, Paul has indicted every single person in the world with rebellion against God. "We have already charged that all, both Jews and Greeks, are under sin" (v. 9). And his sobering conclusion is that when we stand before God the Judge, every mouth will be silenced. No one will mount a defense. Not one excuse will be offered. The whole world—Jew, Gentile, every last one of us—will be held fully accountable to God (v. 19).

Now, strictly speaking, these first two points are not really good news at all. In fact, they're pretty *bad* news. That I have rebelled against the holy and judging God who made me is not a happy thought. But it is an important one, because it paves the way for the good news. That makes sense if you think about it. To have someone say to you, "I'm coming to save you!" is really not good news at all unless you believe you actually need to be saved.

Third, Paul says that God's solution to humanity's sin is the sacrificial death and resurrection of Jesus Christ. Having laid out the bad news of the predicament we face as sinners before our righteous God, Paul turns now to the good news, the *gospel* of Jesus Christ.

"But now," Paul says, in spite of our sin, "*now* the righteousness of God has been manifested apart from the law" (v. 21). In other words, there is a way for human beings to be counted righteous before God instead of unrighteous, to be declared innocent instead of guilty, to be justified instead of condemned. And it has nothing to do with acting better or living a more righteous life. It comes "apart from the law."

So how does it happen? Paul puts it plainly in Romans 3:24. Despite our rebellion against God, and in the face of a hopeless situation, we can be "justified by his grace as a gift, through the redemption that is in Christ Jesus." Through Christ's sacrificial death and resurrection—because of his blood and his life—sinners may be saved from the condemnation our sins deserve.

But there's one more question Paul answers. Exactly how is that good news for me? How do *I* become included in this promised salvation?

Finally, Paul tells his readers how they themselves can be included in this salvation. That's what he writes about through the end of chapter 3 and on into chapter 4. The salvation God has provided comes "through faith in Jesus Christ," and it is "for all who believe" (3:22). So how does this salvation become good news for *me* and not just for someone else? How do *I* come to be included in it? By believing in Jesus Christ. By trusting him and no other to save me. "To the one who does not work but believes in him who justifies the ungodly," Paul explains, "his faith is counted as righteousness" (4:5).

Four Crucial Questions

Now, having looked at Paul's argument in Romans 1–4, we can see that at the heart of his proclamation of the gospel are the answers to four crucial questions:

1. Who made us, and to whom are we accountable?
2. What is our problem? In other words, are we in trouble and why?
3. What is God's solution to that problem? How has he acted to save us from it?
4. How do I—myself, right here, right now—how do *I* come to be included in that salvation? What makes this good news for me and not just for someone else?

We might summarize these four major points like this: God, man, Christ, and response.

Of course Paul goes on to unfold a universe of other promises God has made to those who are saved in Christ, and many of those promises may very appropriately be identified as part of the good news of Christianity, the gospel of Jesus Christ. But it's crucial that we understand, right from the outset, that all those grand promises depend on and flow from this, the heart and fountainhead of the Christian good news. Those promises come only to those who are forgiven of sin through faith in the crucified and risen Christ. That is why Paul, when he presents the heart of the gospel, starts here—with these four critical truths.

The Gospel in the Rest of the New Testament

It's not just Paul who does this. As I read the apostles' writings throughout the New Testament, these are the four questions I see them answering over and over again. Whatever else they might say, these are the issues that seem to lie at the heart of their presentation of the gospel. Contexts change, angles change, words change, and approaches change, but somehow and in some way the earliest Christians *always* seem to get at these four issues: We are accountable to the God who created us. We have sinned against that God and will be judged. *But* God has acted in Jesus Christ to save us, and we take hold of that salvation by repentance from sin and faith in Jesus.

God. Man. Christ. Response.

Let's take a look at some other passages in the New Testament where the gospel of Jesus is summarized. Take Paul's famous words in 1 Corinthians 15, for example:

> Now I would remind you, brothers, of the gospel I preached to you, which you received, in which you stand, and by which you

are being saved, if you hold fast to the word I preached to you—
unless you believed in vain.

For I delivered to you as of first importance what I also
received: that Christ died for our sins in accordance with the
Scriptures, that he was buried, that he was raised on the third
day in accordance with the Scriptures, and that he appeared to
Cephas, then to the twelve. (vv. 1–5)

Do you see the central structure there? Paul is not as expansive as he is in Romans 1–4, but the main contours are still
clear. Human beings are in trouble, sunk in "our sins" and
in need of "being saved" (obviously, though implicitly, from
God's judgment). But salvation comes in this: "Christ died for
our sins . . . was buried . . . was raised." And all this is taken
hold of by "hold[ing] fast to the word I preached to you,"
by believing truly and not in vain. So there it is: God, man,
Christ, response.

Even in the sermons recorded in the book of Acts, this
central framework of the gospel is clear. When Peter tells
the people at Pentecost what they should do in response to
his proclamation of Jesus' death and resurrection, he says,
"Repent and be baptized every one of you, in the name of
Jesus Christ for the forgiveness of your sins" (Acts 2:38).
Again, Peter's appeal is not expansive, and God's judgment
is again implicit, but it's all there nonetheless. The problem:
you need God to forgive your sins, not judge you for them.
The solution: the death and resurrection of Jesus Christ, which
Peter has already talked about at length in the sermon. The
necessary response: repentance and faith, evidenced by the
act of baptism.

In another sermon of Peter's, in Acts 3:18–19, these four crucial truths are obvious again:

> But this is how God fulfilled what he had foretold through all the prophets, saying that his Christ would suffer. Repent, then, and turn to God, so that your sins may be wiped out, that times of refreshing may come from the Lord. (NIV)

Problem: you need your sins wiped out, not judged by God. Solution: Christ suffers. Response: repent and turn to God in faith.

Or consider Peter preaching the gospel to Cornelius and his family:

> We are witnesses of all that he did both in the country of the Jews and in Jerusalem. They put him to death by hanging him on a tree, but God raised him on the third day . . . . To him all the prophets bear witness that everyone who believes in him receives forgiveness of sins through his name. (Acts 10:39–43)

Forgiveness of sins. Through the name of the crucified and risen One. For everyone who believes.

Paul, too, preaches the same gospel in Acts 13:

> Therefore, my brothers, I want you to know that through Jesus the forgiveness of sins is proclaimed to you. Through him everyone who believes is justified from everything you could not be justified from by the law of Moses. (vv. 38–39 NIV)

Once again, the clearly recognizable framework is God, man, Christ, and response. You need God to grant you "forgiveness of sins." That happens "through Jesus," and it happens for "everyone who believes."

Explaining the Core Truths in a Variety of Ways

Obviously this God-man-Christ-response structure is not a slavish formula. The apostles don't necessarily tick the points off like a checklist when they proclaim the gospel. Depending on the context, how long they have to preach, and who is included in their audience, they explain those four points at various lengths. Sometimes one or more of them are even left implicit rather than explicit—especially the fact that it is God to whom we are accountable and from whom we need the gift of forgiveness. But then again, that's a fact that would already have been deep in the minds of the Jews to whom the apostles most often preached.

On the other hand, when Paul speaks to a group of pagan philosophers at the Areopagus, he starts right at the beginning, with God himself. Paul's sermon in Acts 17 is often cited as a model for preaching the good news to a pagan culture. But there's something very interesting and unusual about that sermon. Look at it carefully and you start to realize that Paul doesn't really proclaim the good news of Christ at all, just the bad news!

"Let me tell you about this unknown God to whom you have an altar," he begins, in effect. Then he explains to them in verses 24–28 that there is a God, that this God made the world, and that he calls us to worship him. That established, he turns in verse 29 to explain the concept of sin and its root in worship of created things rather than of God, and he declares that God will judge his hearers by the "man whom he has appointed," a man whom God has raised from the dead (v. 31).

And then he stops! Look at it closely. There's no mention of forgiveness, no mention of the cross, and no promise of salvation—just a declaration of God's demands and a proclamation of the resurrection as proof of his coming judgment! Paul doesn't even mention Jesus' name!

So what's going on here? Does Paul *not* preach the gospel here? Well, no, not right then. There's no gospel, no good news, in his public sermon. The news Paul proclaims is all bad. But look at verses 32–34, where the Bible says that the men wanted to hear Paul again, and that some of them eventually believed. Apparently, Paul preached the *good* news—that sinners could be saved from this coming judgment—at some later time, perhaps publicly, perhaps privately.

Like the other apostles, Paul was perfectly able to present the core truths of the gospel in a variety of ways. But the important thing to understand is that there *were* in fact some core truths of the gospel, and from the sermons and letters preserved to us we have a very good idea of what those core truths were—and are. In Romans, in 1 Corinthians, in the sermons of Acts, and throughout the New Testament, the earliest Christians structured their declaration of the good news around a few critical truths.

First the bad news: God is your Judge, and you have sinned against him. And then the gospel: but Jesus has died so that sinners may be forgiven of their sins if they will repent and believe in him.

2

God the Righteous Creator

Let me introduce you to god. (Note the lowercase *g*.)

You might want to lower your voice a little before we go in. He might be sleeping now. He's old, you know, and doesn't much understand or like this "newfangled" modern world. His golden days—the ones he talks about when you really get him going—were a long time ago, before most of us were even born. That was back when people cared what he thought about things, and considered him pretty important to their lives.

Of course all that's changed now, though, and god—poor fellow—just never adjusted very well. Life's moved on and passed him by. Now, he spends most of his time just hanging in the garden out back. I go there sometimes to see him, and there we tarry, walking and talking softly and tenderly among the roses. . . .

Anyway, a lot of people still like him, it seems—or at least he manages to keep his poll numbers pretty high. And you'd be surprised how many people even drop by to visit and ask for things every once in a while. But of course that's alright with him. He's here to help.

Thank goodness, all the crankiness you read about some-times in his old books—you know, having the earth swallow people up, raining fire down on cities, that sort of thing—all that seems to have faded in his old age. Now he's just a good-natured, low-maintenance friend who's really easy to talk to—especially since he almost never talks back, and when he does, it's usually to tell me through some slightly weird "sign" that what I want to do regardless is alright by him. That really is the best kind of friend, isn't it?

You know the best thing about him, though? He doesn't judge me. Ever, for anything. Oh sure, I know that deep down he wishes I'd be better—more loving, less selfish, and all that—but he's realistic. He knows I'm human and nobody's perfect. And I'm totally sure he's fine with that. Besides, forgiving people is his job. It's what he *does*. After all, he's love, right? And I like to think of love as "never judging, only forgiving." That's the god *I* know. And I wouldn't have him any other way.

Alright, hold on a second. . . . Okay, we can go in now. And don't worry, we don't have to stay long. Really. He's grateful for any time he can get.

Assumptions about God

Okay, okay. That little riff is a bit on the ridiculous side. But I wonder if it's really so far from what many people, even those who call themselves Christians, think about God. For the most part, he's a kind, affable, slightly dazed and needy but very loving grandfather who has wishes but no demands, can be safely ignored if you don't have time for him, and is very, very, *very* understanding of the fact that human beings make mistakes—much more understanding, in fact, than the rest of us are.

It used to be that even if people didn't call themselves Christians, they had a basic understanding of the Bible's teaching about God and his character. It was just part of the atmosphere people breathed, and—much like the apostles did with their fellow Jews—you could make some assumptions about what people knew when you presented the gospel to them.

That's not true anymore, at least in most of the world. I grew up in a small town in East Texas, and most of the time telling someone the gospel amounted to rehearsing a message they'd already heard a thousand times. It was a different world altogether, though, when I started college in New Haven, Connecticut. All of a sudden I was surrounded by people who hadn't grown up hearing about God, and who in fact would challenge me on the idea right from the start. I remember the first time I met someone who greeted my mention of God with, "You've got to be kidding me. You believe that?" And then he laughed.

That episode played itself out dozens of times over the next few years, and I eventually learned to just say, "Yep, I do." But I also learned pretty quickly that I couldn't make assumptions about what people know about God. If I'm going to proclaim the gospel of Jesus Christ today, I'm going to have to start at the very beginning—at God himself.

Of course, you could (and really should!) spend a lifetime studying what God has revealed to us about himself, and you don't have to say everything you know about God in order to present the gospel faithfully. But there are a few basic truths about God that a person *has* to understand in order to grasp what is going on in the good news of Christianity. Think of it as the good news behind the bad news behind the Good News!

There are two main points that we must make clear right from the outset—that God is Creator, and that he is holy and righteous.

God the Creator

The beginning of the Christian message—indeed the beginning of the Christian Bible—is that "God created the heavens and the earth." Everything starts from that point, and like an arrow fired from a badly aimed bow, if you get that point wrong, then everything else that follows will be wrong too.

The book of Genesis opens with the story of God creating the world: its mountains and valleys, animals and fish, birds and reptiles, everything. God created the rest of the universe too: stars and moon, planets and galaxies. All of it came about through his spoken word, and all of it came from *nothing*. It's not as if God took some preexisting material and molded it like clay into all the different things we see in the world. No, Genesis tells us that he spoke, and it was. "Let there be light!" he said. And there was light.

Many biblical passages tell us how creation testifies to God's glory and power. "The heavens declare the glory of God," Psalm 19:1 says. "The sky above proclaims his handiwork." Paul says in Romans 1:20 that God's "invisible attributes, namely, his eternal power and divine nature, have been clearly perceived, ever since the creation of the world, in the things that have been made." If you've ever stood at the edge of a canyon and seen the birds swooping below you and the clouds stretched out over your head, or if you've ever stood in a field and felt a tiny rush of fear as you've watched a thunderstorm roll in over the horizon, then you know what this means. There is something about the grandeur of creation that calls out to the human heart, saying, "You are not all there is!"

The creation story in Genesis expands in both scope and importance with each new day. First is the creation of light, then the sea, then land, then moon and sun, then birds and fishes and animals, and then at the very pinnacle of God's creating work—man and woman.

> Then God said, "Let us make man in our image, after our likeness. And let them have dominion over the fish of the sea and over the birds of the heavens and over the livestock and over all the earth and over every creeping thing that creeps on the earth."

> So God created man in his own image,
>   in the image of God he created him;
>   male and female he created them. (Gen. 1:26–27)

Whatever else you think about the story of creation, the implications of this claim—that God created the world, and especially that God created *you*—are enormous. That the world itself is not ultimate, but that it sprang from the mind, word, and hand of *Someone Else* is a revolutionary idea, especially in our day. Contrary to the nihilism that dominates so much human thinking, it means that everything in the universe has a purpose—including human beings. We are not the result of random chance and genetic mutations, gene reassortments, and chromosomal accidents. We are created! Every one of us is the result of an idea, a plan, and an action of God himself.

And that brings both meaning and responsibility to human life (Gen. 1:26–28).

None of us is autonomous, and understanding that fact is key to understanding the gospel. Despite our constant talk of rights and liberty, we are not really as free as we would like to think. We are created. We are made. And therefore we are owned.

Because he created us, God has the right to tell us how to live. So in the garden of Eden, he told Adam and Eve which trees were theirs to eat from, and which they could not eat (Gen. 2:16–17). It's not that God was acting like a child on a power trip, bossing his little brother around and making arbitrary rules just to see what would happen. No, the Bible tells us that God is good. He knew what was best for his people, and he gave them laws that would preserve and increase their happiness and well-being.

Some understanding of this is absolutely necessary if a person wants to understand the good news of Christianity. The gospel is God's response to the bad news of sin, and sin is a person's rejection of God's Creator-rights over him. Thus the fundamental truth of human existence, the well from which all else flows, is that God created us, and therefore God owns us.

God the Holy and Righteous One

If you had to describe God's character in just a few words, what would you say? That he is loving and good? That he is compassionate and forgiving? All true. When Moses asks God to show him his glory and proclaim his name to him, this is what God said:

The LORD, the LORD, the compassionate and gracious God, slow to anger, abounding in love and faithfulness, maintaining love to thousands, and forgiving wickedness, rebellion and sin. (Ex. 34:6–7 NIV)

How amazing is that! When God wants to tell us his name and show us his glory—which is really to show us his very heart—what does he say? That he is loving and compassionate, slow to anger and abounding in love.

But there's something else in that passage that often gets left out, and it's not quite so comforting. Do you know what God says to Moses right after he says that he is compassionate and loving?

Yet he does not leave the guilty unpunished. (V. 7 NIV)

Take another look at that, because it explodes about 90 percent of what people today *think* they know about God. The loving and compassionate God *does not leave the guilty unpunished.*

A common view of God is that he's much like an unscrupulous janitor. Instead of really dealing with the world's dirt—its sin, evil, and wickedness—he simply sweeps it under the rug, ignores it, and hopes no one will notice. In fact, many people cannot conceive of a God who would do anything else. "God judge sin?" they say. "Punish me for wickedness? Of course he wouldn't do that. It wouldn't be loving."

We'll see later how the seemingly impenetrable contradiction in Exodus 34:6–7—a God who "forgiv[es] wickedness, rebellion and sin" and yet "does not leave the guilty unpunished"—is resolved by the death of Jesus on the cross.

But long before we get there, we must understand that despite all protests to the contrary, God's love does not cancel out his justice and righteousness.

Scripture proclaims over and over that our God is a God of perfect justice and unassailable righteousness. Psalm 11:7 says,

> The LORD is righteous;
> he loves righteous deeds.

Psalm 33:5 declares, "He loves righteousness and justice." And two psalms go so far as to proclaim, "Righteousness and justice are the foundation of your throne" (Pss. 89:14; 97:2)! Do you see what those verses are saying? God's rule over the universe, his sovereign lordship over creation, is founded upon his remaining forever perfectly righteous and just.

That's why the idea of God as an unscrupulous janitor is finally so unsatisfying. It makes God out to be unjust and unrighteous. It makes him a god who simply hides sin—or even hides *from* sin—rather than confronting it and destroying it. It makes him a moral coward.

And who wants a God like that? It's always interesting to watch what happens when people who insist that God would never judge *them* come face to face with undeniable evil. Confronted with some truly horrific evil, *then* they want a God of justice—and they want him *now*. They want God to overlook their own sin, but not the terrorist's. "Forgive me," they say, "but don't you dare forgive him!" You see, nobody wants a God who declines to deal with evil. They just want a God who declines to deal with *their* evil.

Scripture tells us, however, that because he is perfectly just and righteous, God will deal decisively with all evil. Habakkuk 1:13 says,

> Your eyes are too pure to look on evil;
>> you cannot tolerate wrong. (NIV)

To do so would be to renounce the very foundation of his throne. Even more, it would be to renounce his very Self, and that God will not do.

Most people have no problem at all thinking of God as loving and compassionate. We Christians have done a bang-up job convincing the world that God loves them. But if we're going to understand just how glorious and life-giving the gospel of Jesus Christ is, we have to understand that this loving and compassionate God is also holy and righteous, and that he is determined never to overlook, ignore, or tolerate sin.

Including our own. Which of course brings us to the bad news.

3

Man the Sinner

I just paid a parking ticket the other day. It was easy. I read the charge against me, flipped the ticket over, checked the box that said "I plead guilty to the charge," filled out a check for $35 to the Metropolitan Traffic Citation Department, sealed the envelope, and dropped it in the mail.

I'm a convicted criminal.

For some reason, though, even though I checked the "guilty" box, I don't feel terribly guilty. I'm not going to lose any sleep over my walk on the wrong side of the law. I don't feel the need to ask anyone's forgiveness, and now that I think about it, I'm even a little bitter that the ticket was $10 more than the previous one I got.

Why don't I feel bad about breaking the law? I suppose it's because, when you get right down to it, breaking a parking regulation just doesn't strike me as being all that important— or all that heinous. Yes, I'll be sure to drop an extra nickel in the meter next time, but my conscience isn't exactly torn up over the whole thing.

One thing I've noticed over the years is that most people tend to think of sin, especially their own, as not much more than a parking infraction. "Yes of course," we think, "technically sin is a violation of the law handed down by God on high, and all that, but surely he must know there are bigger criminals out there than me. Besides, nobody was hurt, and I'm willing to pay the fine. And come on—there's no need for a whole lot of soul-searching over something like this. Is there?"

Well, I guess not, at least not if you think of sin in that cold way. But according to the Bible, sin is a lot more than just the violation of some impersonal, arbitrary, heavenly traffic regulation. It's the breaking of a relationship, and even more, it is a rejection of God himself—a repudiation of God's rule, God's care, God's authority, and God's right to command those to whom he gave life. In short, it is the rebellion of the creature against his Creator.

What Went Wrong

When God created human beings, his intention was that they would live under his righteous rule in perfect joy, worshipping him, obeying him, and thereby living in unbroken fellowship with him. As we saw in the last chapter, he created man and woman in his own image, meaning that they were to be like him, to be in relationship with him, and to declare his glory to the world. Further, God had a job for humans to do. They were to be his vice-regents, ruling his world under him. "Be fruitful and multiply," God told them, "and fill the earth and subdue it and have dominion over the fish of the sea and over the birds of the heavens and over every living thing that moves on the earth" (Gen. 1:28).

Man and woman's rule over creation was not ultimate, however. Their authority was not their own; it was given to them by God. So even as Adam and Eve exercised dominion over the world, they were to remember that they were subject to God and under his rule. He had created them, and therefore he had the right to command them.

The tree of the knowledge of good and evil, which God planted in the center of the garden, was a stark reminder of that fact (Gen. 3:17). When Adam and Eve looked at that tree and saw its fruit, they would remember that their authority was limited, that they were creatures, and that they were dependent on God for their very lives. They were only the stewards. He was the King.

When Adam and Eve bit into the fruit, therefore, they weren't just violating some arbitrary command, "Don't eat the fruit." They were doing something much sadder and much more serious. They were rejecting God's authority over them and declaring their independence from him. Adam and Eve wanted to be, as the Serpent promised them, "like God," so both of them seized on what they thought was an opportunity to shed the vice-regency and take the crown itself. In all the universe, there was only one thing God had not placed under Adam's feet—God himself. Yet Adam decided this arrangement was not good enough for him, and so he rebelled.

The worst of it, though, is that by disobeying God's command, Adam and Eve made a conscious decision to reject him as their King. They knew what the consequences would be if they disobeyed him. God had told them in no uncertain terms that if they ate the fruit, they would "surely die," which meant above all that they would be cast away from his presence and become his enemies, rather than his friends and joyful subjects (Gen. 2:17). But they didn't care. Adam and Eve traded their favor with God for the pursuit of their own pleasure and their own glory.

The Bible calls this disobedience of God's commands—whether in word, thought, or deed—"sin." Literally, the word means "missing the mark," but the biblical meaning of sin is much deeper. It's not as if Adam and Eve were trying very hard to keep God's command and just missed the bull's-eye by a few degrees. No, the fact is that they were shooting in the opposite direction! They had goals and desires that were categorically opposed to what God desired for them, and so they sinned. They deliberately violated God's command, broke their relationship with him, and rejected him as their rightful Lord.

The consequences of Adam and Eve's sin were disastrous for them, their descendants, and the rest of creation. They themselves were cast out of the idyllic garden of Eden. No longer would the earth willingly and joyfully present its fruits and treasures to them. They would have to work, hard and painfully, to get them. Even worse, God executed the promised sentence of death upon them. They didn't physically die right away, of course. Their bodies continued to live, lungs breathing, hearts beating, limbs moving. But their spiritual life, the one that matters most, ended immediately. Their fellowship with God was broken, and thus their hearts shriveled, their minds filled up with selfish thoughts, their eyes darkened to the beauty of God, and their souls became sere and arid, utterly void of that spiritual life that God gave them in the beginning, when everything was good.

Not Just Them, but Us

The Bible tells us that it is not just Adam and Eve who are guilty of sin. We all are. Paul says in Romans 3:23, "All have sinned and fall short of the glory of God." And just a few paragraphs earlier he says, "None is righteous, no, not one" (3:10).

The gospel of Jesus Christ is full of stumbling stones, and this is one of the largest. To human hearts that stubbornly think of themselves as basically good and self-sufficient, this idea that human beings are fundamentally sinful and rebellious is not merely scandalous. It is revolting.

That's why it is so absolutely crucial that we understand both the nature and the depth of our sin. If we approach the gospel thinking that sin is something else or something less than what it really is, we will badly misunderstand the good news of Jesus Christ. Let me give you a few examples of how Christians often misunderstand sin.

Confusing Sin with Sin's Effects

It's become fashionable lately to present the gospel by saying that Jesus came to save humanity from an innate sense of guilt or meaninglessness or purposelessness or emptiness. Now of course those things really are problems, and many people feel them deeply. But the Bible teaches that humanity's fundamental problem—the thing from which we need to be saved—is not meaninglessness or disintegration in our lives, or even a debilitating sense of guilt. Those are merely symptoms of a deeper and much more profound problem: our sin. What we must understand is that the predicament we're in is a predicament of our own making. *We* have disobeyed God's word. *We* have ignored his commands. *We* have sinned against him.

To talk about salvation being from meaninglessness or purposelessness without tracing those things down to their root in sin may make the medicine go down easier, but it is the wrong medicine. It allows a person to continue thinking of himself as a victim and never really deal with the fact that he himself is the criminal, unrighteous and deserving of judgment.

Reducing Sin to Broken Relationship

Relationship is an important category in the Bible. Human beings were *made* to live in fellowship with God. What we must remember, however, is that it was a specific *kind* of relationship in which they were to live—not the relationship between two equals, where law, judgment, and punishment are out of view, but the relationship between a King and his subjects.

Many Christians talk about sin as if it were merely a relational tiff between God and man, and what is needed is for us simply to apologize and accept God's forgiveness. That image of sin as lovers' quarrel, though, distorts the relationship in which we stand to God. It communicates that there is no broken law, no violated justice, no righteous wrath, no holy judgment— and therefore, ultimately, no need for a substitute to bear that judgment, either.

The Bible's teaching is that sin is indeed a breaking of relationship with God, but that broken relationship consists in a rejection of his kingly majesty. It's not *just* adultery (though it is that); it is also rebellion. Not *just* betrayal, but also treason. If we reduce sin to a mere breaking of relationship, rather than understanding it as the traitorous rebellion of a beloved subject against his good and righteous King, we will never understand why the death of God's Son was required to address it.

Confusing Sin with Negative Thinking

Another misunderstanding of sin is to say that it's just a matter of negative thinking. We saw that in some of the quotes in the introduction to this book. Get rid of your old wineskins! Think bigger! God wants to show you his incredible favor, if you'll just get rid of all those negative mind-sets that hold you back!

Now that's a compelling message to self-reliant people who want to believe they can take care of their sin all by themselves. That's probably why men who proclaim that message have managed to build some of the largest churches in the world. The formula is pretty easy, really. Just tell people that their sin is no deeper than negative thinking and that it's holding them back from health, wealth, and happiness. Then tell them that if they'll just think more positively about themselves (with God's help, of course), they'll be rid of their sin and get rich, to boot. Bingo! Instant megachurch!

Sometimes the promised goal is money, sometimes health, sometimes something else entirely. But however you spin it, to say that Jesus Christ died to save us from negative thoughts about ourselves is reprehensibly unbiblical. In fact, the Bible teaches that a big part of our problem is that we think too *highly* of ourselves, not too lowly. Stop and think about it for a moment. How did the Serpent tempt Adam and Eve? He told them they were thinking too negatively about themselves. He told them they needed to think more positively, to extend their grasp, to reach toward their full potential, to be like God! In a word, he told them to think bigger.

Now how'd that work out for them?

Confusing Sin with Sins

There is a huge difference between understanding yourself to be guilty of sin*s*, and knowing yourself to be guilty of *sin*. Most people have no problem at all admitting that they've committed sin*s* (plural), at least so long as they can think about those sins as isolated little mistakes in an otherwise pretty good life— a parking ticket here or there on an otherwise clean record.

Sin*s* don't shock us much. We know they are there, we see them in ourselves and others every day, and we've gotten pretty used to them. What is shocking to us is when God shows us the *sin* that runs to the very depths of our hearts, the deep-running deposits of filth and corruption that we never knew existed in us and that we ourselves could never expunge. That's how the Bible talks about the depth and darkness of our sin—it is *in* us and *of* us, not just *on* us.

On the second floor of the National Museum of Natural History in Washington, there is what is said to be the largest flawless quartz sphere in the entire world. The sphere is a little bigger than a basketball, and there is a not a single visible scratch, pockmark, or discoloration on the entire thing. It is perfect. People often think human nature is like that quartz sphere. Yes, every now and then we may smear it up with dirt and mud, but underneath the grime it remains as pristine as ever, and all we really need to do is wipe it clean in order to restore its brilliance.

The Bible's picture of human nature, though, is not so pretty. According to Scripture, the sphere of human nature is not pristine at all, and the mud is not just smeared on the outside. On the contrary, we are shot through with sin. The cracks, mud, filth, and corruption go all the way to the center.

We are, as Paul said, "by nature children of wrath" (Eph. 2:3). We are included in Adam's guilt and corruption (Romans 5). Jesus taught this, too: "Out of the heart come evil thoughts, murder, adultery, sexual immorality, theft, false witness, slander" (Matt. 15:19). The sinful words you speak and sinful actions you do are not just isolated incidents. They rise out of the evil of your own heart.

Every part of our human existence is corrupted by sin and under its power. Our understanding, our personality, our feelings and emotions, and even our will are all enslaved to sin. So Paul says in Romans 8:7, "The mind that is set on the flesh is hostile to God, for it does not submit to God's law; indeed, it cannot." What a shocking and frightening statement! So thorough is sin's rule over us—our minds, understanding, and will—that we see God's glory and goodness, and we *inevitably* turn away from it in disgust.

It's not enough to say that Jesus came to save us from sin*s*, if what we mean by that is that he came to save us from our isolated mistakes. It's only when we realize that our very nature is sinful—that we are indeed "dead in our trespasses and sins," as Paul says (Eph. 2:1, 5)—that we see just how good the news is that there is a way to be saved.

God's Active Judgment against Sin

One of the most frightening statements in all the Bible is in Romans 3:19. It comes at the end of Paul's indictment of all humanity—first the Gentile, then the Jew—as being under sin and utterly unrighteous before God. Here's what Paul says, as the grand conclusion of the matter: "Every mouth

[will] be silenced and the whole world held accountable to God" (NIV).

Can you even begin to imagine what that will mean? To stand before God and to have no explanation, no plea, no excuse, no case? And what does it mean to be "held accountable to God"? The Bible is very clear, as we saw in the last chapter, that God is righteous and holy, and therefore he will not excuse sin. But what will it mean for God to deal with sin, to judge it and punish it?

Romans 6:23 says, "The wages of sin is death." In other words, the payment we earn for our sins is to die. That's not just physical death, either. It is spiritual death, a forceful separating of our sinful, wretched selves from the presence of the righteous and holy God. The prophet Isaiah describes it like this:

> Your iniquities have made a separation
>   between you and your God,
> and your sins have hidden his face from you
>   so that he does not hear. (Isa. 59:2)

Sometimes people talk about this as if it is just the passive, quiet absence of God. But it's more than that. It is God's active judgment against sin, and the Bible says it will be terrifying. Look at how the book of Revelation describes what the end will be like on the day of God's right and good judgment. The seven angels will "pour out on the earth . . . the wrath of God," and "all the tribes of the earth will wail on account of him" (Rev. 16:1; 1:7). They will call out to the mountains and the rocks, "Fall on us and hide us from the face of him who is seated on the throne, and from the wrath of the Lamb, for the great day of their wrath has come, and who can stand?" (Rev. 6:16–17). They will see Jesus, the King of kings and Lord of lords, and they will cower, for "he will tread the winepress of the fury of the wrath of God the Almighty" (Rev. 19:15).

The Bible teaches that the final destiny for unrepentant, unbelieving sinners is a place of eternal, conscious torment called "hell." Revelation describes it as a "lake of fire and sulfur," and Jesus says it is a place of "unquenchable fire" (Rev. 20:10; Mark 9:43).

Given how the Bible talks about hell and warns us against it, I do not understand the impulse some Christians seem to have to explain it in a way that makes it sound more tolerable. When Revelation speaks of Jesus treading the winepress of the fury of the wrath of God Almighty, when Jesus himself warns of the "unquenchable fire . . . where their worm does not die and the fire is not quenched" (Mark 9:43, 48), my incredulous question is, *Why* would any Christian have an interest in making that sound *less* horrific? *Why on earth* would we comfort sinners with the thought that maybe hell will not be so bad after all?

We Didn't Just Make This Up

The images the Bible uses to talk about God's judgment against sin are truly horrifying. It's really no wonder the world reads the Bible's descriptions of hell and calls Christians "sick" for believing them.

But that misses the point. It's not as if we just make these ideas up ourselves. We Christians don't read, believe, and talk about hell because we somehow enjoy the thought of it. God forbid. No, we talk about hell because, finally, we believe the

Bible. We believe it when it says that hell is real, and we believe it with tears when it says that people we love are in danger of spending eternity there.

This is the Bible's sobering verdict on us. There is not one of us righteous, not even one. And because of that, one day every mouth will be silenced, every wagging tongue stopped, and the whole world will be held accountable to God.

But . . .

4

Jesus Christ
the Savior

But. I think that must be the most powerful word a human being can speak. It's small, but it has the power to sweep away everything that has gone before it. Coming after bad news like what we just heard, it has the power to lift the eyes and restore hope. More than any other word that can be spoken by a human tongue, it has the ability to change everything.

- The plane went down. *But* no one was hurt.
- You have cancer. *But* it is easily treatable.
- Your son was in a car wreck. *But* he's fine.

Sadly, sometimes the *but* doesn't come. Sometimes the sentence stops, and all we get is the bad news. Yet those moments only magnify for us the times when the *but* does come. And they are glorious.

Thank God the bad news of human sin and God's judgment is not the end of the story. If the Bible had ended with Paul's declaration that the whole world will stand, silenced, before the judgment throne of God, there would be no hope for us at all. There would be only despair. But (there it is again!) thank God there is more!

You are a sinner destined to be condemned. *But* God has acted to save sinners just like you!

A Word of Hope

Mark begins his account of Jesus' life with the words, "The beginning of the gospel of Jesus Christ, the Son of God." From the very beginning, Mark and the other early Christians knew that the coming of Jesus Christ was God's good news to a world destroyed and dead at the feet of sin. In the wake of sin's dark devastation, the coming of Jesus was his piercing, thundering announcement that now everything had changed!

Even in the garden of Eden, God had given Adam and Eve a word of hope—some good news in the midst of their despair. It wasn't much, just a hint really, a phrase tacked onto the end of God's sentence against the Serpent.

> He shall bruise your head,
>   and you shall bruise his heel. (Gen. 3:15)

But it was something. God wanted Adam and Eve, rebels though they were, to know that the story was not over. Here was some gospel, some good news in the midst of the cataclysm.

The rest of the Bible tells the story of how this tiny seed of good news germinated, sprouted, and grew. For thousands of years, God prepared the world through law and prophecy for his stunning *coup de grace* against the Serpent in the life, death, and resurrection of Jesus Christ. When it was all over, the guilt Adam had inflicted on his entire race would be defeated, the death God pronounced over his own creation would die, and hell would be brought to its knees. The Bible is the story of God's counteroffensive against sin. It is the grand narrative of how God made it right, how he is making it right, and how he will one day make it right finally and forever.

Fully God, Fully Man

All the gospel writers begin their accounts of Jesus' life by showing that he was no ordinary man. Matthew and Luke tell the story of an angel coming to a young virgin named Mary and telling her that she would be with child. Incredulous at the news, Mary asks, "How will this be, since I am a virgin?" The angel explains, "The Holy Spirit will come upon you, and the power of the Most High will overshadow you; therefore the child to be born will be called holy—the Son of God" (Luke 1:34–35). John begins his story with an even more astonishing statement: "In the beginning" (words that point back strongly to Gen. 1:1) "was the Word, and the Word was with God, and the Word was God. . . . The Word became flesh and dwelt among us" (John 1:1, 14).

All of this—Jesus' birth to a virgin, the title "Son of God," John's assertion that "the Word was God" together with his announcement that "the Word became flesh"—is meant to teach us who Jesus is.

Put simply, the Bible tells us that Jesus is both completely human and completely God. This is a crucial point to understand about him, for it is only the fully human, fully divine Son of God who can save us. If Jesus were just another man—like us in every respect, including our fallenness and sin—he would no more be able to save us than one dead man can save another. But because he is the Son of God, without sin and equal in every divine perfection to God the Father, he is able to defeat death and save us from our sin. In the same way, it is also critical that Jesus be truly one of us—that is, fully human—so that he can rightly represent us before his Father. As Hebrews 4:15 explains, Jesus is able "to sympathize with our weaknesses" because he "in every respect has been tempted as we are, yet without sin."

The Messiah King—Here!

When Jesus began his ministry, he proclaimed a fantastic message: "The time has come! The kingdom of God is at hand. Repent and believe the good news!"

Word of this man preaching that the kingdom of God had come spread quickly throughout the country, and excited crowds soon surrounded Jesus to hear this "good news" that he was proclaiming. But what was so exciting about it?

For centuries, through his law and his prophets, God had foretold a time when he would once and for all put an end to the world's evil and rescue his people from their sin. He would sweep away all resistance and establish his rule, his "kingdom," over all the earth. Even more, God had promised that he would establish his kingdom in the person of a messianic King, one in the royal line of the great King David. In 2 Samuel 7:11, God promised David that one of his sons would rule on his throne forever. And the prophet Isaiah said of this kingly son:

> He will be called
>> Wonderful Counselor, Mighty God,
>> Everlasting Father, Prince of Peace.
> Of the increase of his government and peace
>> there will be no end.

> He will reign on David's throne
> > and over his kingdom,
> establishing and upholding it
> > with justice and righteousness
> > from that time on and forever. (Isa. 9:6–7 NIV)

So you can imagine the excitement that greeted Jesus when he began announcing that the kingdom of heaven had come. It meant that the long-awaited Davidic Messiah was finally here!

The Gospel writers are insistent that this Davidic King is none other than Jesus himself. Luke records the words of the angel announcing Jesus' birth to Mary:

> He will be great and will be called the Son of the Most High. And the Lord God will give to him the throne of his father David, and he will reign over the house of Jacob forever, and of his kingdom there will be no end. (Luke 1:32–33)

Matthew begins his book with a genealogy that traces Jesus' ancestry directly back to King David, and then on back to Abraham himself. Fascinatingly, Matthew stylizes his genealogy, dividing it into three generations of fourteen. And fourteen, as any good Jew would have known, was the number arrived at by adding up the values of the three Hebrew letters *D-V-D*, "David." Matthew, like all the other Christians, practically screams as he begins his story about Jesus, "King! King! King!"

Unexpected Good News—If You Can Get in on It

The New Testament then tells the story of how King Jesus inaugurated the rule of God on earth and began rolling back the curse of sin. The kingdom Jesus inaugurated, though, looked nothing like what the Jews expected or wanted. They wanted a messiah who would establish an earthly, political kingdom that would overthrow and supplant the Roman Empire, the ruling power of the day. Yet here was Jesus not at all looking for an earthly crown, but preaching, teaching, healing the sick, forgiving sin, raising the dead, and telling the Roman governor in no uncertain terms, "My kingdom is not of this world" (John 18:36).

That's not to say his kingdom would *never* be of this world. Just a little earlier Jesus had said to the high priest, "You will see the Son of Man seated at the right hand of Power, and coming with the clouds of heaven" (Mark 14:62), and in Revelation 21 we read of him reigning over a new heavens and new earth radically transformed by his power and released from its bondage to sin.

Now all that is undeniably good news—if you can get in on it. But then we're back to the problem of our sin, aren't we? Unless something happens to remove the guilt of our disobedience and rebellion against God, we are still separated from him and destined not for the joys of a new heaven and new earth, but for the eternal punishment of hell.

But here is where the good news of Christianity gets really, really good. You see, King Jesus came not only to inaugurate the kingdom of God, but also to bring sinners into it by dying in their place and for their sin, taking their punishment on himself and securing forgiveness for them, making them righteous in God's sight, and qualifying them to share in the inheritance of the kingdom (Col. 1:12).

A Suffering King?

"Behold, the Lamb of God, who takes away the sin of the world!" That's what John the Baptist, the camel-skin-clad, locust-eating prophet, said when he saw Jesus coming toward him (John 1:29). What did he mean? The Lamb of God? Taking away the sin of the world?

Every first-century Jew would have known immediately what John meant by "the Lamb of God taking away sin." It was a reference to the Jewish festival of the Passover, a memorial of God's miraculous deliverance of the Israelites from slavery in Egypt some fifteen hundred years earlier.

As judgment against the Egyptians, God had sent ten plagues on them, and each time the Egyptian king hardened his heart and refused to let the people go. The last of the plagues was the most terrible of all. God told the Israelites that on an appointed night, an angel of death would sweep through the land of Egypt, killing every firstborn child and animal in the country. That horrible judgment would include the Israelites, too—unless they carefully obeyed God's instructions. Each family, God told them, was to take a lamb without any defect or blemish, and kill it. Then using a branch of hyssop, they were to put some of the blood around the doorframe of their house. Then, God promised, when the angel of death saw the blood, he would "pass over" that house and spare it the judgment of death.

The Passover feast—and especially the Passover lamb—became a powerful symbol of the idea that the penalty of death for one's sins could be paid by the death of another. This idea of "penal substitution," in fact, grounded the entire system of Old Testament sacrifices. On the annual Day of Atonement, the high priest went into the center of the temple, known as the Most Holy Place, and killed an unblemished animal as payment for the people's sins. Year after year this happened, and year after year the penalty for the people's sins was deferred yet again by the blood of the lamb.

It took time, but eventually the followers of Jesus realized that his mission was not just to inaugurate the kingdom of God, but to do so by dying as a substitutionary sacrifice for his people. Jesus was not just King, they realized. He was suffering King.

Jesus himself knew from the very beginning that his mission was to die for the sins of his people. The angel had announced at his very birth that "he will save his people from their sins" (Matt. 1:21), and Luke tells us that "when the days drew near for him to be taken up, he set his face to go to Jerusalem" (Luke 9:51). Jesus foretold his death many times in the gospels, and when Peter foolishly tried to stand in his way, Jesus rebuked him: "Get behind me, Satan! You are a hindrance to me" (Matt. 16:23). Jesus' face was set like flint toward Jerusalem—and therefore toward his death.

Jesus also understood the significance and purpose of his death. In Mark 10:45, he says, "The Son of Man came not to be served but to serve, and to give his life as a ransom for many." And in Matthew 26:28, as he shared a last supper with his disciples, he took a cup of wine and declared, "Drink of it, all of you, for this is my blood of the covenant, which is poured out for many for the forgiveness of sins" (Matt. 26:27–28). "I lay down my life for the sheep," he said in another place. "No one takes it from me, but I lay it down of my own accord" (John 10:15, 18). Jesus knew why he was going to die. Out of love for his people he willingly laid down his life, the Lamb of God slain so his people could be forgiven.

Taught by the Holy Spirit, the early Christians also understood what Jesus had accomplished on the cross. Paul described it like this: "Christ redeemed us from the curse of the law by becoming a curse for us" (Gal. 3:13–14). And in another place he explained, "God made him who had no sin to be sin for us, so that in him we might become the righteousness of God" (2 Cor. 5:21 NIV). Peter wrote, "Christ also suffered once for sins, the righteous for the unrighteous, that he might bring us to God" (1 Pet. 3:18). And, "He himself bore our sins in his body on the tree, that we might die to sin and live to righteousness. By his wounds you have been healed" (1 Pet. 2:24).

Do you see what these Christians were saying about the significance of Jesus' death? They were saying that when Jesus died, it was not the punishment for his own sins that he endured. (He didn't have any!) It was the punishment for his people's sins! As he hung on the cross at Calvary, Jesus bore all the horrible weight of the sin of God's people. All their rebellion, all their disobedience, all their sin fell on his shoulders. And the curse that God had pronounced in Eden—the sentence of death—struck.

That is why Jesus cried out in agony, "My God, my God, why have you forsaken me?" (Matt. 27:46). God his Father, who is holy and righteous, whose eyes are too pure even to look on evil, looked at his Son, saw the sins of his Son's people resting on his shoulders, turned away in disgust, and poured out his wrath on his own Son. Matthew writes that darkness covered the land for about three hours while Jesus hung on the cross. That was the darkness of judgment, the weight of the Father's wrath falling on Jesus as he bore his people's sins and died in their place.

Isaiah prophesied about this seven centuries before it happened:

> Surely he has borne our griefs
>   and carried our sorrows;
> yet we esteemed him stricken,
>   smitten by God, and afflicted.
> But he was wounded for our transgressions;
>   he was crushed for our iniquities;
> upon him was the chastisement that brought us peace,
>   and with his stripes we are healed. (Isa. 53:4–5)

Do you see the significance of this? Ultimately, it means that *I'm* the one who should have died, not Jesus. *I* should have been punished, not he. And yet he took my place. He died for me.

They were my transgressions, but his wounds. My iniquities, but his chastisement. My sin, his sorrow. And his punishment bought my peace. His stripes won my healing. His grief, my joy.

His death, my life.

The Heart of the Gospel

Sadly, this doctrine of substitution is probably the one part of the Christian gospel that the world hates most. People are simply disgusted at the idea of Jesus being punished for someone else's sin. More than one author has called it "divine child abuse." And yet to toss substitutionary atonement aside is to cut out the heart of the gospel. To be sure, there are many pictures in Scripture of what Christ accomplished with his death: example, reconciliation, and victory, to name three. But underneath them all is the reality to which all the other images point—penal substitution. You simply cannot leave it out, or even downplay it in favor of other images, or else you litter the landscape of Scripture with unanswered questions. Why the sacrifices? What did that shedding of blood accomplish? How can God have mercy on sinners without destroying justice? What can it mean that God forgives iniquity and transgression and sin, and yet by no means clears the guilty (Ex. 34:7)? How can a righteous and holy God justify the ungodly (Rom. 4:5)?

The answer to all these questions is found at the cross of Calvary, in Jesus' substitutionary death for his people. A righteous and holy God can justify the ungodly because in Jesus' death, mercy and justice were perfectly reconciled. The curse was righteously executed, and we were mercifully saved.

He Has Risen

Of course, all this is true—and good news—only because King Jesus the crucified is no longer dead. He rose from the grave. All the doubt that crashed in on the disciples as Jesus died was erased in a moment when the angel said to the women, "Why do you seek the living among the dead? He is not here, but has risen" (Luke 24:5–6).

If Christ had remained dead like any other "savior" or "teacher" or "prophet," his death would have meant nothing more than yours or mine. Death's waves would have closed over him just as they do over every other human life, every claim he made would have sunk into nothingness, and humanity would still be without hope of being saved from sin. But when breath entered his resurrected lungs again, when resurrection life electrified his glorified body, everything Jesus claimed was fully, finally, unquestionably, and irrevocably vindicated.

Paul exults in Romans 8 over Jesus' resurrection and what it means for believers:

> Who shall bring any charge against God's elect? It is God who justifies. Who is to condemn? Christ Jesus is the one who died—more than that, who was raised—who is at the right hand of God, who indeed is interceding for us. (Rom. 8:33–34)

What an amazing thought—that the man Jesus now sits in splendor at the right hand of his Father in heaven, reigning as the King of the universe! Not only so, but he is even now interceding for his people, even as we await his final and glorious return.

But all this raises one more question, doesn't it? Just who are "his people"?

5

Response—Faith and Repentance

I started trying to teach my son to swim very early on. It was a chore. A year or so old at the time, the little guy didn't like getting water in his face in the bathtub, much less this massive ocean of a pool he was staring at now. At first, "teaching him to swim" meant getting him to splash around a bit on the top step, and maybe putting his lips in the water enough to blow some bubbles if he was feeling really brave.

Eventually I convinced him to walk around with me in the shallow end, with a death-grip around my neck, of course. Once we mastered that, it was time for the Big Show—Jumping Off the Side. Fulfilling my God-given duty as a daddy, I lifted him out of the pool, stood him on the side, and said, "Come on, jump!"

I think, at that moment, my one-year-old son wrote me off as a crazy man. The look on his face, in about two seconds, went from confusion to dawning understanding, to amused rejection, to outright contempt. He frowned and said, "No. I go see Mommy." Again acting faithfully on my solemn responsibility as a father, I refused to surrender, chased him down and eventually convinced him (with various bribes) to come back to the pool. And so we came to the moment of truth.

I jumped into the water again and stood in front of him with my arms outstretched, watching him bob up and down in his swimmy-diaper as one-year-olds do when they kind of want to jump but not really. "Come on, kiddo," I said. "I'm right here. I'll catch you, I promise!" He looked at me half skeptically, did one more little wind-up, bouncing at the knees, and then fell into the pool with what was more a flop than a jump.

And I caught him.

After that, we were off to the races. "Doot 'gain, daddy! Doot 'gain!" And so commenced half an hour of jump, catch, lift, reset, jump, catch, lift, reset.

When it was over, my wife and I started to worry that maybe our son had gotten a bit *too* comfortable with the water. What if he wandered out to the pool when no one was there with him? Would he remember all the times he'd safely jumped into the water and decide he had this pool thing whipped? Would he jump again?

Over the next few days we watched him around the pool, and what we saw both comforted me as a parent and touched me deeply as a father. Never once did my little boy think about jumping into the water—at least not unless I was standing underneath him with my arms out, promising to catch him. And then he would fly!

You see, despite all his apparent successes, my son's trust was never in his own ability to handle the water. It was in his father, and in his father's promise, "Come on, kiddo. Jump. I promise I'll catch you."

Introducing Faith and Repentance

Mark tells us that Jesus began his ministry by preaching, "The time is fulfilled, and the kingdom of God is at hand; repent and believe in the gospel" (Mark 1:15). That command—repent and believe—is what God requires of us in response to the good news of Jesus.

Throughout the New Testament, this is what we see the apostles calling people to do. Jesus called on his listeners to repent and believe the good news. Peter, at the end of his sermon on the day of Pentecost, told the people to "repent and be baptized every one of you in the name of Jesus" (Acts 2:38).[1] Paul explained his ministry in Acts 20:21, saying, "I have declared to both Jews and Greeks that they must turn to God in repentance and have faith in our Lord Jesus" (NIV). And in 26:18, he recounts how Jesus himself had sent him

> to open their eyes, so that they may turn from darkness to light and from the power of Satan to God [that is, repent], that they may receive forgiveness of sins and a place among those who are sanctified by faith in me.

Faith and repentance. This is what marks out those who are Christ's people, or "Christians." In other words, a Christian is one who turns away from his sin and trusts in the Lord Jesus Christ—and nothing else—to save him from sin and the coming judgment.

Faith Is Reliance

Faith is one of those words that's been misused for so long that most people have no idea what it really means. Ask someone on the street to describe faith, and while you might get some

---

[1] Being baptized in the name of Jesus is an expression of faith in him.

respectful-sounding words, the heart of the matter will most likely be that faith is belief in the ridiculous against all evidence.

One year I was watching the Macy's Thanksgiving Day Parade on television with my oldest son. The event's theme was "Believe!" and the focal point, suspended above the reviewing stand, was what the anchors were calling a Believe-o-meter. Every time a new float came by, or a band played, or dancers danced in their elf costumes, the needle on the Believe-o-meter bounced a little higher. Of course, the highlight of the parade was when Santa Claus himself rode in—his sleigh fashioned inexplicably in the shape of a majestic goose—and the Believe-o-meter went wild! What with the music, the dancing, the confetti, and the screaming kids—and screaming adults, for that matter—an alien visitor would surely have concluded that yes, Virginia, these people really *do* believe this.

My six-year-old, God bless him, thought the whole thing was uproariously silly.

But that's what the world thinks now about faith. It's a charade, a fun and comforting game that people are free to engage in if they wish, but with no real connection to the actual world. Children believe in Santa Claus and the Easter bunny. Mystics believe in the power of stones and crystals. Crazy people believe in fairies. And Christians, well, they believe in Jesus.

Read the Bible, though, and you'll find that faith is nothing like that caricature. Faith is not believing in something you can't prove, as so many people define it. It is, biblically speaking, *reliance*. A rock-solid, truth-grounded, promise-founded *trust* in the risen Jesus to save you from sin.

Paul tells us about the nature of faith in Romans 4, in his discussion about Abraham. Here's how he describes Abraham's faith:

> In hope he believed against hope, that he should become the father of many nations, as he had been told, "So shall your offspring be." He did not weaken in faith when he considered his own body, which was as good as dead (since he was about a hundred years old), or when he considered the barrenness of Sarah's womb. No distrust made him waver concerning the promise of God, but he grew strong in his faith as he gave glory to God, fully convinced that God was able to do what he had promised. (Rom. 4:18–21)

Despite all that was working against God's promise—Abraham's age, his wife's age and barrenness—Abraham believed what God had said. He trusted in God without wavering and relied on him to accomplish his promises. Abraham's was not a perfect faith, of course; Ishmael's birth to Hagar proves that Abraham at first tried to rely on his own schemes to fulfill God's promises. But having repented of that sin, Abraham in the end put his faith in God. He relied on him, as Paul says, "fully convinced that God was able to do what he had promised."

The gospel of Jesus Christ calls us to do the very same thing—to put our faith in Jesus, rely on him, and trust him to do what he has promised to do.

Faith for a Righteous Verdict

But what exactly are we relying on Jesus for? To put it simply, we are relying on him to secure for us a righteous verdict from God the Judge, rather than a guilty one.

Let me explain. The Bible teaches that the greatest need of every human being is to be found righteous in God's sight, rather than wicked. When the judgment comes, we desperately need the verdict pronounced over us to be "righteous" rather than "condemned." That is what the Bible calls being "justified"—it is God's declaration that we are righteous in his sight, rather than guilty.

And how do we secure this righteous verdict? The Bible tells us plainly that it won't be by asking God to look at our own lives. No, that would be a fool's move. If God is ever to count us righteous, he will have to do it on the basis of something other than our own sinful record. He'll have to do it on the basis of someone *else's* record, someone who is standing as a substitute for us. That's where faith in Jesus comes in. When we put our faith in Jesus, we are relying on him to stand as our substitute before God, in both his perfect life and his penalty-paying death for us on the cross. In other words, we are trusting that God will substitute Jesus' record for ours, and therefore declare us to be righteous (Rom. 3:22).

You might think of it like this: When we trust Jesus to save us, we become united to him, and a magnificent exchange takes place. All our sin, rebellion, and wickedness is imputed (or credited) to Jesus, and he dies because of it (1 Pet. 3:18). And at the same time, the perfect life Jesus lived is imputed to us, and we are declared righteous. God looks at us, and instead of seeing our sin, he sees Jesus' righteousness.

This is what Paul means when he writes in Romans 4 that God "counts righteousness" to us apart from our own works, and that our sins are "covered" (vv. 5, 7). Most importantly, it's what Paul means when he says, shockingly, that God "justifies the ungodly" (v. 5)! God does not declare us righteous because we are ourselves righteous. And thank God that is true, because none of us would meet that standard! No, God declares us righteous because by faith, we are clothed with Christ's righteous life. God saves us by pure grace, not because of anything we have done, but solely because of what *Jesus* has done for us.

The prophet Zechariah makes this point with a beautiful image of Joshua the high priest being given new clothes. Here's what Zechariah writes:

> Then he showed me Joshua the high priest standing before the angel of the LORD, and Satan standing at his right side to accuse him. The LORD said to Satan, "The LORD rebuke you, Satan! The LORD, who has chosen Jerusalem, rebuke you! Is not this man a burning stick snatched from the fire?"
>
> Now Joshua was dressed in filthy clothes as he stood before the angel. The angel said to those who were standing before him, "Take off his filthy clothes."
>
> Then he said to Joshua, "See, I have taken away your sin, and I will put rich garments on you."
>
> Then I said, "Put a clean turban on his head." So they put a clean turban on his head and clothed him, while the angel of the LORD stood by. (Zech. 3:1–5 NIV)

Those rich, clean, new clothes did not belong to Joshua. Nor did that clean turban. All that belonged to Joshua himself were the filthy clothes in which he stood, the very ones Satan was about to point to in derision and accusation. No, the righteousness Joshua enjoyed before God was not his own. It was given to him by another.

That is true for us as Christians, too. Our righteousness before God is not our own. It is given to us by Jesus. God looked at his Son and saw our sin, and he looks at us and sees Jesus' righteousness. As the song says,

> God the just is satisfied,
> to look on Him and pardon me.[2]

Faith Alone

When you realize just how dependent you are on Jesus for your salvation—his death for your sin, his life for your righteousness—you understand why the Bible is so insistent that salvation comes *only* through faith in him. There is no other way, no other savior, nothing and no one else in the world on which we can rely for salvation, including our own efforts.

Every other religion in human history rejects this idea that we are justified by faith alone. Instead, other religions assert that salvation is won through moral effort, good deeds, and somehow balancing one's account by accruing enough merit to outweigh one's evil. That's not surprising, really. It's very human to think—and even to *insist*—that we can contribute to our own salvation.

We are all such self-reliant people, aren't we? We're convinced of our own self-sufficiency, and we resent any insinuation that we are what we are because of somebody else's intervention. Think of how you would feel if someone said about your job or something else you value, "Yeah, you didn't earn that. You only have it because somebody *gave* it to you." And yet that's exactly the case when it comes to our salvation before

---

[2] "Before the Throne of God Above," Charitie L. Bancroft, 1863.

God. It is given to us as a gift of grace, and we don't contribute anything at all—not our own righteousness, not our own payment for our sins, and certainly not any good works that balance the account (Gal. 2:16).

Putting your faith in Christ means that you utterly renounce any other hope of being counted righteous before God. Do you find yourself trusting in your own good works? Faith means admitting that they are woefully insufficient, and trusting Christ alone. Do you find yourself trusting what you understand to be your good heart? Faith means acknowledging that your heart is not good at all, and trusting Christ alone. To put it another way, it means jumping off the edge of the pool and saying, "Jesus, if you don't catch me, I'm done. I've no other hope, no other savior. Save me, Jesus, or I die."

That is faith.

Repentance, the Flip Side of the Coin

Jesus' message to his listeners was, "Repent and believe in the gospel" (Mark 1:15). If faith is turning to Jesus and relying on him for salvation, repentance is the flip side of that coin. It is turning away from sin, hating it, and resolving by God's strength to forsake it, even as we turn to him in faith. So Peter told the on-looking crowd, "Repent, then, and turn to God, so that your sins may be wiped out" (Acts 3:19 NIV). And Paul tells everyone "that they should repent and turn to God" (Acts 26:20).

Repentance is not just an optional plug-in to the Christian life. It is absolutely crucial to it, marking out those who have been saved by God from those who have not.

I have known many people who would say something like, "Yes, I've accepted Jesus as Savior, so I'm a Christian. But I'm just not ready to accept him as Lord yet. I have some things to work through." In other words, they claimed that they could have faith in Jesus and be saved, and yet not repent of sin.

If we understand repentance rightly, we'll see that the idea that you can accept Jesus as Savior but not Lord is nonsense. For one thing, it just doesn't do justice to what Scripture says about repentance and its connection with salvation. For example, Jesus warned, "Unless you repent, you will all likewise perish" (Luke 13:3). The apostles, when they heard Peter's story about the conversion of Cornelius, praised God for granting to the Gentiles "repentance that leads to life" (Acts 11:18), and Paul speaks of "repentance that leads to salvation" in 2 Corinthians 7:10.

Moreover, to have faith in Jesus is, at its core, to believe that he really is who he says he is—the crucified and risen King who has conquered death and sin, and who has the power to save. Now how could a person believe all that, trust in it, and rely on it, and yet at the same time say, "But I don't acknowledge that you are King over *me*"? That doesn't make any sense. Faith in Christ carries in itself a renunciation of that rival power that King Jesus conquered—sin. And where that renunciation of sin is not present, neither is genuine faith in the One who defeated it.

It is as Jesus said in Matthew 6:24: "No one can serve two masters, for either he will hate the one and love the other, or he will be devoted to the one and despise the other." To put one's faith in King Jesus is to renounce his enemies.

Repentance, Not Perfection but Taking Sides

Now none of that means that a Christian will never sin. Repenting of sin doesn't necessarily mean that you stop sinning—certainly not altogether, and often not in particular areas, either. Christians are still fallen sinners even after God gives us new spiritual life, and we will continue to struggle with sin until we are glorified with Jesus (see, e.g., Gal. 5:17; 1 John 2:1). But even if repentance doesn't mean an immediate end to our sinning, it does mean that we will no longer live at peace with our sin. We will declare mortal war against it and dedicate ourselves to resisting it by God's power on every front in our lives.

Many Christians struggle hard with this idea of repentance because they somehow expect that if they genuinely repent, sin will go away and temptation will stop. When that doesn't happen, they fall into despair, questioning whether their faith in Jesus is real. It's true that when God regenerates us, he gives us power to fight against and overcome sin (1 Cor. 10:13). But because we will continue to struggle with sin until we are glorified, we have to remember that genuine repentance is more fundamentally a matter of the heart's attitude toward sin than it is a mere change of behavior. Do we hate sin and war against it, or do we cherish it and defend it?

One writer put this truth beautifully:

> The difference between an unconverted and a converted man is not that the one has sins and the other has none; but that the one takes part with his cherished sins against a dreaded

God, and the other takes part with a reconciled God against his hated sins.[3]

So whose side do you take—your sin's or your God's?

Real Change, Real Fruit

When a person genuinely repents and believes in Christ, the Bible says that he is given new spiritual life. "As for you, you were dead in your transgressions and sins," Paul says. "But because of his great love for us, God, who is rich in mercy, made us alive with Christ even when we were dead in transgressions" (Eph. 2:1, 4–5 NIV). When that happens, our life changes—not immediately, not quickly, not even necessarily steadily. But it does change. We begin to bear fruit.

The Bible says that Christians are to be marked by the same kind of love, compassion, and goodness that characterized Jesus himself. True Christians will perform "deeds in keeping with their repentance," Paul says (Acts 26:20). "Each tree is known by its own fruit," Jesus said. "For figs are not gathered from thornbushes, nor are grapes picked from a bramble bush" (Luke 6:44). In other words, when people are given new spiritual life, they begin to do the kinds of things that Jesus did. They begin to live like Jesus lived and bear good fruit.

One thing we must be constantly on guard against is any thought that those fruits are the cause of our salvation. There is always a danger that when we begin to see fruit in our lives, we'll subtly begin to rely on that fruit for our salvation, instead

[3]William Arnot, *Laws from Heaven for Life on Earth* (London: T. Nelson and Sons, 1884), 311.

of on Christ. Guard against that temptation, Christian. Realize that the fruit you bear is merely that—the fruit of a tree already made good by God's grace in Christ. To rely on your own Christian fruit to secure God's favor is ultimately to shift your faith from Jesus to yourself. And that is no salvation at all.

Where Will You Point?

When you stand before God at the judgment, I wonder what you plan to do or say in order to convince him to count you righteous and admit you to all the blessings of his kingdom? What good deed or godly attitude will you pull out of your pocket to impress him? Will you pull out your church attendance? Your family life? Your spotless thought life? The fact that you haven't done anything really heinous in your own eyes? I wonder what you'll hold up before him while saying, "God, on account of *this*, justify me!"

I'll tell you what every Christian whose faith is in Christ alone will do, by God's grace. They will simply and quietly point to Jesus. And this will be their plea: "O God, do not look for any righteousness in my own life. Look at your Son. Count me righteous not because of anything I've done or anything I am, but because of him. He lived the life I should have lived. He died the death that I deserve. I have renounced all other trusts, and my plea is him alone. Justify me, O God, because of Jesus."

6

The Kingdom

On the entrance to the parking lot of my church, there is a bronze plaque with the immortal words of the missionary Jim Elliot: "He is no fool who gives what he cannot keep to gain what he cannot lose." I love that quote because it captures so well both the cost and the reward of being a Christian.

There's no doubt that becoming a Christian is a costly thing (Luke 14:28). But it's also true that the rewards of being a Christian are inexpressibly awesome. Forgiveness of sins, adoption as God's children, relationship with Jesus, the gift of the Holy Spirit, freedom from sin's tyranny, the fellowship of the church, the final resurrection and glorification of the body, inclusion in God's kingdom, the new heavens and new earth, eternity in God's presence, seeing his face—all these are the promises God makes to us in Christ. No wonder Paul quoted Isaiah, saying,

> No eye has seen,
>   no ear has heard,
> no mind has conceived
>   what God has prepared for those who love him.
>   (1 Cor. 2:9 NIV)

The Christian life is not just about making sure you avoid God's wrath. Far from it! It's about being in a *right* relationship with God, and ultimately enjoying him forever. That is to say, it's about gaining what we cannot lose—becoming a citizen of his eternal kingdom.

From the moment a person becomes a believer in Jesus Christ, everything in his life changes forever. I know, I know—sometimes it doesn't feel like that. There's no heavenly confetti, and there are no trumpets, no angels singing (at least not that we can hear), but it's true nonetheless. *Everything* changes. God has "delivered us," Paul says, "from the dominion of darkness and transferred us to the kingdom of his beloved Son" (Col. 1:13).

What Is the Kingdom of God?

The kingdom of God is an important theme in the New Testament. Jesus himself preached about it constantly, saying, "Repent, for the kingdom of heaven is near." Acts 28:31 summarizes Paul's ministry like this: "Boldly and without hindrance he preached the kingdom of God and taught about the Lord Jesus" (NIV). The author of Hebrews exults in the fact that believers in Christ are "receiving a kingdom that cannot be shaken" (Heb. 12:28), and Peter encourages his readers with the thought of being richly welcomed into "the eternal kingdom of our Lord and Savior Jesus Christ" (2 Pet. 1:11). Then in the book of Revelation, all the hosts of heaven erupt in praise: "Now the salvation and the power and the kingdom of our God and the authority of his Christ have come" (Rev. 12:10).

But what is this kingdom, exactly? Is it a realm, a piece of real estate that God has special authority over? Is it the church?

Is it here now, or is it something we're waiting for, something that will come in the future? For that matter, who exactly is in the kingdom of God? Doesn't God's rule extend over everyone, regardless of whether he or she believes in Jesus? Aren't we all in the kingdom, and can't we all—regardless of whether we're Christians or not—work toward the establishment of the kingdom?

Let's try to get at some of these questions by noticing a few things that Scripture teaches about the kingdom of God.

God's Redemptive Reign

First, the kingdom of God is God's redemptive rule over his people. *Kingdom* is one of those words that brings along with it very strong connotations, and in this case those connotations tend to confuse. Usually when we think about a kingdom, we think of a particular plot of land with a well-defined set of borders. *Kingdom* is a geographical word for most of us. That's not the case in the Bible, though. Biblically speaking, the kingdom of God is best understood as more a king*ship* than a king*dom* as we usually use that word. God's kingdom is therefore God's rule, reign, and authority (Ps. 145:11, 13).

There's another crucial word we need to add to our definition, though. As the Bible talks about it, God's kingdom is not just his rule and reign. It is his *redemptive* rule and reign; it's the loving sovereignty he exercises over *his own people*.

Of course it's true that not one square inch of the universe, not one single person, is independent of God's rule or somehow outside his authority. He created all, he rules over all, and he will judge all. But when the Bible uses the phrase "kingdom of God," it usually refers very specifically to God's rule over his own people, over those who have been saved through Christ. Thus Paul talks about Christians being transferred from the dominion of darkness into the kingdom of Christ (Col. 1:12–13), and he is very careful to point out that the wicked will not inherit the kingdom of God (1 Cor. 6:9).

The kingdom of God, then, simply defined, is God's redemptive rule, reign, and authority over those redeemed by Jesus.

A Kingdom Come

Second, the kingdom of God is here. When Jesus began his earthly ministry, he preached a stunning message: "Repent, for the kingdom of heaven is at hand" (Matt. 3:2). Actually, you could translate that as, "Repent, for the kingdom of heaven has come!"

We've already seen what a stunning claim Jesus was making with those words. The Jews had for centuries been waiting, hoping, and praying for the dawning of the kingdom, for the day when God's rule would be established on the earth and his people would finally be vindicated. And now here was Jesus—this Nazarene carpenter-turned-teacher—telling them that the day they'd been waiting for was here.

Not only so, but he was claiming that the kingdom of God had been inaugurated *in him*! So in Matthew 12:28, when the Pharisees accuse Jesus of driving out demons in the name of Satan, Jesus rebukes them and makes a staggering claim: "If it is by the Spirit of God that I cast out demons, then the kingdom of God has come upon you." Do you see what he's saying? Clearly, Jesus *was* driving out demons, and he was doing so by the Spirit of God. What he was claiming was that, finally, God's promised deliverance of his people had begun. The kingdom had come.

What an awesome thought that is! Jesus' incarnation was much more than just a kind visit from the Creator. It was the launching of God's full and final counteroffensive against all the sin, death, and destruction that had entered the world when Adam fell.

You can see the war happening all over the story of Jesus' life in the New Testament. King Jesus goes alone into the wilderness to face Satan—the one who had tempted Adam and thrown the world into corruption so many years earlier—and decisively defeats him! He touches the eyes of a man born blind, and light enters for the very first time. He stares into the sad blackness of a tomb and cries out "Lazarus, come forth!" and death feels its grip on humanity begin to weaken as the dead man walks out.

And then above all, of course, sin itself was defeated when Jesus cried out on the cross, "It is finished!" And death's grip finally failed entirely when the angel said—with a smile, I'm sure—"Why do you seek the living among the dead? He is not here, but has risen" (Luke 24:5–6). Step by step, blow by blow, Jesus was decisively rolling back the effects of the fall. The rightful King of the world had come, and all that stood in the way of the establishment of his kingdom—sin, death, hell, Satan—was being decisively overcome.

What this means is that many of the blessings of the kingdom are already ours. So Jesus tells his disciples that he will send them "another Comforter," the Holy Spirit, who will guide them, convict them of sin, and sanctify them. In the same way, Christians know even now what it is to have been adopted into God's family and to be reconciled to him. Paul even says that in God's eyes, we are already raised up and seated with Christ (Eph. 2:6).

That is an incredibly encouraging truth. But there's something else, something equally important, that we must understand.

A Kingdom Not Yet Complete

Third, the kingdom of God is not yet completed, and it will not be completed until King Jesus returns. Despite all that Jesus did to overthrow the powers of evil, he did not fully and finally establish God's rule on the earth—at least not yet. The strong man was bound, but not destroyed. Evil was defeated, but not annihilated, and the kingdom of God was inaugurated, but not brought to full and final completion.

Jesus spoke of a future day when the kingdom would finally be consummated. On that day, he said, the angels "will weed out of his kingdom everything that causes sin and all who do evil. . . . Then the righteous will shine like the sun in the kingdom of their Father" (Matt. 13:41–43 NIV). He also looks forward at the Last Supper to the day when he would drink the fruit of the vine again with his disciples: "I tell you I will not drink again of this fruit of the vine until that day when I drink it new with you in my Father's kingdom" (Matt. 26:29).

Paul, too, looks longingly forward to the resurrection of the dead in eternity (1 Corinthians 15), and he tells the Ephesians that they have been sealed by the Holy Spirit "who is the guarantee of our inheritance *until we acquire possession of it*" (Eph. 1:14). Later he says that God has saved us "so that *in the coming ages* he might show the immeasurable riches of his grace in kindness toward us in Christ Jesus" (Eph. 2:7). Peter too speaks of a "salvation ready to be revealed in the last time" (1 Pet. 1:5), and the author of Hebrews tells his readers that they are "strangers and exiles on the earth" (Heb. 11:13) and that they should look forward to "the city that has foundations, whose designer and builder is God" (v. 10).

The great hope for Christians, the thing for which we long and to which we look for strength and encouragement, is the day when our King will part the skies and return to establish his glorious kingdom, finally and forever. That glorious moment is when everything in this world will be set right, when justice will finally be done, evil overthrown forever, and righteousness established once and for all. God promises:

> Behold, I will create
> > new heavens and a new earth.
> The former things will not be remembered,
> > nor will they come to mind. . . .
> I will rejoice over Jerusalem
> > and take delight in my people;
> the sound of weeping and of crying
> > will be heard in it no more. (Isa. 65:17–19 NIV)

And in that day, the prophet tells us,

> They shall not hurt or destroy
> > in all my holy mountain;
> for the earth shall be full of the knowledge of the LORD
> > as the waters cover the sea. (Isa. 11:9)

I used to think as a child that the Christian's destiny was to spend eternity in a never-ending disembodied church service.

That was a scary thought! But it was entirely wrong. God intends to create for his people a new world, free of sin and death and sickness. War will end, oppression will cease, and God will dwell with his people forever. Never again will any of God's people suffer death, and never again will tears burn our eyes at a graveside. Never again will an infant live but a few days and then die. Never again will we mourn, or hurt, or weep. Never again will we long for home. For as Revelation tells us, God himself will wipe every tear from our eyes, and we will, finally, see his face!

Really, what do you say in response to all that? One thing, I think: Oh, Lord Jesus, come quickly!

I'm always a little amazed when I see people talk about all these promises—the new heavens and new earth, the heavenly city into which nothing evil ever enters, the world emptied of death, war, and oppression, the resurrected people of God living joyfully before his face forever—and then they look up from those promises and say, "Okay, let's go make that happen!"

The fact is that we as human beings are not going to be able to bring about the establishment and consummation of God's kingdom. Despite all our best—and genuinely good—efforts to make the world a better place, the kingdom promised in the Bible will only come about when King Jesus himself returns to make it happen.

That's a crucial thing to remember, for at least a couple of reasons. First, it protects us from a wrong and ultimately deceiving optimism about what we will be able to accomplish in this fallen world. Christians will certainly be able to bring about some changes in society. It's happened before in history, and I have no reason to doubt that it is happening in places even now and that it will happen again in the future. Christians have done and can still do massive good in the world—good that will commend God and Jesus Christ to the world.

But I think the biblical story line forces us to recognize that until Christ returns, our social and cultural victories will always be tenuous, never permanent. Christians will never bring about the kingdom of God. Only God himself can do that. The heavenly Jerusalem *comes down from heaven*; it is not built from the ground up.

Even more importantly, remembering that the kingdom will only be established when Jesus returns rightly centers our hopes, our affection, and our longing on Jesus himself. Instead of looking to some human power, some human action, some human authority, or even our own effort to set everything right, we look to heaven and cry out with the apostle John, "Even so, come, Lord Jesus!" Our longing for his return increases, our prayers to him grow more fervent, and our love for him deepens. In short, our desires and hopes center firmly—and rightly—not so much on the kingdom as on the kingdom's King.

A Response to the King

Fourth, inclusion in the kingdom of God depends entirely on one's response to the King. Jesus could not have been clearer about this. Over and over, he makes a person's response to him and his message the single determining factor in whether that person would be included in his kingdom. Think about the story of the rich young ruler. "What must I do to inherit eternal life?" the man asks. And Jesus' answer, finally, is "Follow me," which for that man meant turning away from his trust in his own wealth and believing in Jesus (Mark 10:17, 21).

Time after time, Jesus says that God will draw a bright line through the middle of humanity, separating the saved from the unsaved. And the one thing that will make the difference between the two is how they responded to King Jesus. That's the point of the story of the sheep and the goats in Matthew 25. In the end, the difference between "Come" and "Depart from me" is how each person responded to Jesus as he was presented by his "brothers," that is, his people.

And, of course, what makes it possible for us to be Jesus' people in the first place is his death for us on the cross. That's the really astonishing thing about Jesus, not just that he was King or that he inaugurated a kingdom of love and compassion. Really, that's not that astonishing at all; every Jew knew that was going to happen some day. No, what was really astonishing about the gospel of Jesus was that this King *died* to save his people, that the Messiah turned out to be a *crucified* Messiah.

The Jews had hoped for centuries for a messianic King to come and rescue them. They also had hopes for a suffering Servant of the Lord (prophesied by Isaiah), and they even had a vague expectation of a divine "son of man" who would appear at the end of the age (Daniel). What they never fathomed, though, was that all three of these figures would turn out to be the same man! No one ever pulled those three strands together—at least not until Jesus.

Jesus, however, not only declared himself to be the fulfillment of Israel's messianic hopes (that is, the King), but also constantly referred to himself as the divine "Son of Man" from Daniel 7. Even more, Jesus said of the Son of Man that he came "to give his life as a ransom for many" (Mark 10:45), which points unmistakably to the suffering Servant of the Lord in Isaiah 53:10.

Do you see what Jesus was claiming? He was saying that he himself fulfilled—all at the same time—the roles of the Davidic Messiah, the Suffering Servant of Isaiah, and Daniel's Son of Man! Jesus took the divine nature of the Son of Man, joined to it the substitutionary suffering of the Servant, and finally combined all that with his messianic role. By the time Jesus finished gathering together all the threads of Jewish hope, this King was infinitely more than the earthly revolutionary the Jews were hoping for. He was the divine Servant-King, who would suffer and die for his people to win their salvation, make them righteous in his Father's eyes, and bring them gloriously into his kingdom.

In light of all that, it's no wonder that Jesus makes entrance into his kingdom depend solely on whether a person repents of sin and trusts in him and his atoning work on the cross. When Jesus talks about "the gospel of the kingdom," his point is not just that the kingdom has come. It is that the kingdom has come *and* you can be included in it if you are united to Me, the King, by faith that I alone can save you from your sin.

Therefore, being a citizen of Christ's kingdom is not a matter of just "living a kingdom life" or "following Jesus' example" or "living like Jesus lived." The fact is, a person can be a self-professed "Jesus-follower" or "kingdom-life liver" and still be outside the kingdom. You can live like Jesus lived all you want, but unless you've come to the crucified King in repentance and faith, relying on him alone as the perfect sacrifice for your sin and your only hope for salvation, you're neither a Christian nor a citizen of his kingdom.

The way to be included in Christ's kingdom is to come to the King, not just hailing him as a great example who shows us a better way to live, but humbly trusting him as the crucified and risen Lord who alone can release you from the sentence of death. At the end of the day, the only way into the kingdom is through the blood of the King.

A Call to Live for the King

Fifth, to be a citizen of the kingdom is to be called to live the life of the kingdom. In Romans 6, Paul calls Christians to recognize that they have been rescued from the dominion of sin and brought into the kingdom of God.

> We were buried therefore with him by baptism into death, in order that, just as Christ was raised from the dead by the glory of the Father, we too might walk in newness of life.
>
> For if we have been united with him in a death like his, we shall certainly be united with him in a resurrection like his. We know that our old self was crucified with him in order that the body of sin might be brought to nothing, so that we would no longer be enslaved to sin. For one who has died has been set free from sin. Now if we have died with Christ, we believe that we will also live with him. We know that Christ, being raised from the dead, will never die again; death no longer has dominion over him. For the death he died he died to sin, once for all, but the life he lives he lives to God. So you also must consider yourselves dead to sin and alive to God in Christ Jesus. (Rom. 6:4–11)

When we are brought by faith into the kingdom of God, the Holy Spirit gives us a new life. We become citizens of a new kingdom, and subjects of a new King. Because of that we also have a new obligation to obey that king, to live in a way that honors him. That's why Paul says:

> Let not sin therefore reign in your mortal body, to make you obey its passions. Do not present your members to sin as instruments for unrighteousness, but present yourselves to God as those who have been brought from death to life. (Rom. 6:12–13)

Until Christ returns, we his people continue to live in this sinful age, and our King calls us to live a life that is worthy of the kingdom to which he has called us (1 Thess. 2:12), to "shine like stars" in a crooked and depraved generation (Phil. 2:15 NIV). It's not at all that living the life of the kingdom brings us into the kingdom. It's that once we have been brought into the kingdom through faith in the King, we find ourselves with a new master, a new law, a new charter, a new life—and therefore we begin to *want* to live the life of the kingdom.

The Bible tells us that in this age, the life of the kingdom is worked out primarily in the church. Did you ever think about that? The church is where God's kingdom is made visible in this age. Look at Ephesians 3:10–11:

> [God's] intent was that now, through the church, the manifold wisdom of God should be made known to the rulers and authorities in the heavenly realms, according to his eternal purpose which he accomplished in Christ Jesus our Lord. (NIV)

The church is the arena in which God has chosen, above all, to showcase his wisdom and the glory of the gospel. As many have put it before, the church is the outpost of God's kingdom in this world. It's not correct to say that the church *is* the kingdom of God. As we've seen, there's much more to the kingdom than that. But it *is* right to say that the church is where we *see* the kingdom of God manifested in this age.

Do you want to see what the kingdom of God looks like, at least before it's made perfect? Do you want to see the life of the kingdom lived out in this age? Look at the church. That's where God's wisdom is displayed, where people who were formerly alienated are reconciled and united because of Jesus, and where God's Holy Spirit is at work remaking and rebuilding human lives. It's where God's people learn to love one another, to bear one another's burdens and sorrows, to weep together and rejoice together, and to hold one another accountable. Of course it's not perfect, but the church is where the life of the kingdom is lived and showcased to a world desperately in need of salvation.

Pressing On through Darkness

Of course, it's just that desperate need of the world to be saved that makes living as a citizen of Christ's kingdom in this age so hard. To the world, Christians are threatening, and it has always been that way. In the days of the early church, the declaration "Jesus is Lord!" was a seditious and blasphemous rejection of the emperor's authority, and they killed Christians for saying it. Today, the declaration "Jesus is Lord" is an intolerant and bigoted rejection of pluralism, and the world reviles us for it.

Never in Scripture is the life of the kingdom—the struggle to remain faithful to the King—said to be easy. Jesus promised that his followers would face persecution, that they would be reviled and mocked and even killed. But even in the midst of all that, we Christians press on because we know that there is laid up for us in God's presence an inheritance beyond anything we could ever imagine.

In the last book of J. R. R. Tolkien's magnificent epic *The Lord of the Rings*, the heroes of the story come to the darkest part of their journey. They've traveled a thousand miles and come finally to the evil land that has been their goal, but for several different reasons, everything seems lost now. Yet in that darkest moment, one of the heroes, Sam, looks into the black sky. Here's what Tolkien writes:

> Far above the mountains in the west, the night-sky was still dim and pale. There, peeping among the cloud-wrack above a dark tor high up in the mountains, Sam saw a white star twinkle for a while. The beauty of it smote his heart, as he looked up out of the forsaken land, and hope returned to him. For like a shaft, clear and cold, the thought pierced him that in the end the Shadow was a small and passing thing: there was light and high beauty forever beyond its reach.

That is one of my favorite moments in the story, because it is right there that Tolkien, who himself professed faith in Christ, points us to where we find the courage to press on through darkness. It comes from hope. It comes from knowing that our present sufferings are indeed a small and passing thing, and that, as Paul said, they truly are not worth comparing to the glory that will be revealed in us when our King returns.

7

Keeping the Cross at the Center

At one point in John Bunyan's *Pilgrim's Progress*, the hero of the story, Christian, finds himself talking with two sketchy fellows named Formalist and Hypocrisy. Like Christian himself, they insist, they are on their way to the Celestial City, and they're quite certain they'll make it because many in their country have gone this way before.

Of course, the names give it away. Formalist and Hypocrisy aren't going to make it to the city at all.

The first time Christian sees the two men, they are tumbling over the wall that runs alongside the narrow path Christian is on. He of course recognizes that this is problematic, since he knows that the only legitimate way into the narrow path was through the Wicket Gate, which in the story symbolizes repentance and faith in the crucified Christ.

Christian, never afraid to go straight to the point, presses the two men on the matter: "Why came you not in at the gate?" The men quickly explain that the people of their country think the gate is too far away, and so they decided long ago "to make a short-cut of it." Besides, they argue,

> If we make it onto the path, what's it matter which way we got in? If we are in, we are in. You are on the path, and you came in at the gate; we are on the path, and we climbed over the wall. So how are you any better off than we are?

Christian warns the men that the Lord of the city has decreed that everyone who enters the Celestial City must enter the narrow path through the gate, and he shows them a scroll he was given there, which he must present at the gate of the city in order to gain entrance. "I imagine," Christian says, "that you lack this, because you didn't come in at the gate."

Bunyan's point was to show that the only way to salvation is through the Wicket Gate—that is, through repentance and faith. It's not enough to be navigating the path of the Christian life. If a person doesn't come in through that gate, he is not truly a Christian.

A Bigger, More Relevant Gospel?

That's an old story, but it's an even older point that Bunyan was making. Since the very beginning of time, people have been trying to save themselves in ways that make sense to *them*, rather than listening and submitting to God. They have been trying to figure out how to get salvation to work—how to get the *gospel* to work—apart from the Wicket Gate, that is, apart from the cross of Jesus Christ.

That is no less true in our own day. Indeed I believe one of the greatest dangers the body of Christ faces today is the temptation to rethink and rearticulate the gospel in a way that makes its center something other than the death of Jesus on the cross in the place of sinners.

The pressure to do that is enormous, and it seems to come from several directions. One of the main sources of pressure is the increasingly common idea that the gospel of forgiveness of sin through Christ's death is somehow not "big" enough—that it doesn't address problems like war, oppression, poverty, and injustice, and really "isn't terribly important," as one writer put it, when it comes to the real problems of this world.

Now, I think that charge is altogether false. All those problems are, at their root, the result of human sin, and it is folly to think that with a little more activism, a little more concern, a little more "living the life that Jesus lived," we can solve those problems. No, it is the cross alone that truly deals once and for all with sin, and it is the cross that makes it possible for humans to be included in God's perfect kingdom at all.

Nevertheless, the pressure to find a "bigger," more "relevant" gospel seems to have taken hold of a great many people. Again and again, in book after book, we see descriptions of the gospel that end up relegating the cross to a secondary position. In its place are declarations that the heart of the gospel is that God is remaking the world, or that he has promised a kingdom that will set everything right, or that he is calling us to join him in transforming our culture. Whatever the specifics, the result is that over and over again, the death of Jesus in the place of sinners is assumed, marginalized, or even (sometimes deliberately) ignored.

Three Substitute Gospels

This decentering of the cross is happening subtly among evangelical Christians, it seems to me, in several different ways. A number of "bigger and better" gospels have been advocated in recent years, and each of them seems to be gaining a significant following. Insofar as these "bigger" gospels make their center something other than the cross, however, I would argue that they are really less than the gospel, or no gospel at all. Let me give you three examples of this.

"Jesus Is Lord" Is Not the Gospel

One of the most popular of these "bigger" gospels is the claim that the good news is simply the proclamation that "Jesus is Lord." Much as a herald might enter a city and declare, "Caesar is Lord," Christians are to herald the good news that it is Jesus who rules, and that he is in the process of reconciling the entire world to himself and bringing it under his reign.

Of course, the declaration that "Jesus is Lord" is absolutely, magnificently true! And that declaration of Jesus' lordship is essential to the gospel message. So Paul says in Romans 10:9 that the person who confesses that "Jesus is Lord" will be saved, and in 1 Corinthians 12:3 he says that it is only by the Spirit of God that someone can affirm that truth.

But surely it's not correct to say that the declaration "Jesus is Lord" is the whole sum and substance of the Christian good news. We've already seen how the earliest Christians said much more than that when they proclaimed the gospel. Yes, in Acts 2, Peter preached, "Let all the house of Israel therefore know for certain that God has made him both Lord and Christ, this Jesus whom you crucified" (v. 36). But before and after that statement is a full explanation of what Jesus' lordship *meant*. It meant that this Lord had been crucified, buried, and resurrected, and it also meant that his death and resurrection, above all, had accomplished the "forgiveness of sins" for those who would repent and believe in him. Peter did not just declare that Jesus is Lord. He proclaimed that this Lord had acted on behalf of his people to save them from God's wrath against their sin.

It should be obvious by now that to say simply that "Jesus is Lord" is really not good news at all if we don't explain how Jesus is not just Lord but also Savior. Lordship implies the right to judge, and we've already seen that God intends to judge evil. Therefore, to a sinner in rebellion against God and against his Messiah, the proclamation that Jesus has become Lord is terrible news. It means that your enemy has won the throne and is now about to judge you for your rebellion against him.

For that news to be good and not simply terrifying, it would have to include a way for your rebellion to be forgiven, a way for you to be reconciled to this One who has been made Lord. That's exactly what we see in the New Testament—not just the proclamation that Jesus is Lord, but that this Lord Jesus has been crucified so that sinners may be forgiven and brought into the joy of his coming kingdom. Apart from that, the declaration that "Jesus is Lord" is nothing but a death sentence.

Creation-Fall-Redemption-Consummation Is Not the Gospel

Many Christians have outlined the story of the Bible using the four words *creation, fall, redemption, consummation.*

Actually that outline is a really good way to summarize the Bible's main story line. God creates the world, man sins, God acts in the Messiah Jesus to redeem a people for himself, and history comes to an end with the final consummation of his glorious kingdom. From Genesis to Revelation, that's a great way to remember the Bible's basic narrative. In fact, when you understand and articulate it rightly, the creation-fall-redemption-consummation outline provides a good framework for a faithful presentation of the biblical gospel.

The problem, though, is that creation-fall-redemption-consummation has been used wrongly by some as a way to place the emphasis of the gospel on God's promise to renew the world, rather than on the cross. Thus the creation-fall-redemption-consummation "gospel" is too often presented as being something like this:

> The gospel is the news that in the beginning God created the world and everything in it. It was originally very good, but human beings rebelled against God's rule and threw the world into chaos. The relationship between humans and God was broken, as were people's relationships with each other, with themselves, and with their world. After the fall, however, God promised to send a King who would redeem a people for himself and reconcile creation to God once again. That promise began to be fulfilled with the coming of Jesus Christ, but it will be finally completed, or consummated, when King Jesus returns.

Everything in that paragraph, of course, is true. But what I wrote there is not the gospel. Just like the proclamation that "Jesus is Lord" is not good news unless there is a way to be forgiven of your rebellion against him, so the fact that God is remaking the world is not good news unless you can be included in that.

Of course it's perfectly fine to use creation-fall-redemption-consummation as a way to explain the good news of Christianity. In fact, the categories "creation" and "fall" line up almost exactly with our categories of "God" and "man." The crucial point, though, comes at the category of "redemption." That's where, in order truly to proclaim the gospel, we must carefully explain the death and resurrection of Jesus and the response God requires of sinners. If we say merely that God is redeeming a people and remaking the world, but do not say *how he is doing so* (through the death and resurrection of Jesus) and *how a person can be included in that redemption* (through repentance from sin and faith in Jesus), then we have not proclaimed the good news. We have simply told the narrative of the Bible in broad outline and left sinners with their faces pressed against the window, looking in.

Cultural Transformation Is Not the Gospel

The idea of seeing culture transformed through the work of Christians seems lately to have captured the minds of many evangelicals. I think that is a noble goal, and I also think that the effort to resist evil in society, whether personal or systemic, is a biblical one. Paul tells us that we are to "do good to everyone, and especially to those who are of the household of faith" (Gal. 6:10). Jesus tells us we are to care for our neighbors, which includes those who are outsiders (Luke 10:25–37). And he also tells us, "Let your light shine before others, so that they may see your good works and give glory to your Father who is in heaven" (Matt. 5:16).

Many transformationalists go further than that, however, finding the mandate to "redeem the culture" in the very fabric of the biblical story. If God is in the business of remaking the world, they argue, then it is our responsibility to join him in that work, to gather the building materials of the kingdom, and to take significant strides toward the establishment of God's reign in our neighborhoods, our cities, our nations, and our world. "We must do what we see God doing," they say.

Let me go ahead and lay all my thoughts on the table. I have some serious biblical and theological reservations about the cultural transformation paradigm. I'm not convinced that Scripture places efforts at cultural transformation in quite the position of priority that many transformationalists call for. That's for several reasons. For one thing, I don't think the cultural mandate in Genesis is given to the people of God as such; I think it's given to human beings as a whole. I also don't think the general trajectory of human culture, either in Scripture or in history, is in a godward direction; instead, I think the trajectory of human culture on the whole, though not in every particular, is judgment-ward (see Revelation 17–19). So I think the optimism of many transformationalists about the possibility of "changing the world" is misleading and therefore will prove discouraging.

All that, however, is an enormous biblical-theological discussion, and it's not my main concern here. I actually think it's possible to be a committed transformationalist and at the same time be committed to keeping the cross of Jesus at the very center of the biblical story and of the good news. After all, it is the *forgiven* and *redeemed* people of God whom he would use to accomplish the transformation, and forgiveness and redemption take place only through the cross.

My main concern is rather something that I hope my evangelical transformationalist friends would heartily agree with. It is that far too often among some transformationalists, cultural redemption subtly becomes the great promise and point of the gospel—which of course means that the cross, deliberately or not, is pushed out of that position. You can see this happening in book after book calling for a greater emphasis on cultural transformation. The highest excitement and joy are ignited by the promise of a reformed culture rather than by the work of Christ on the cross. The most fervent appeals are for people to join God in his work of changing the world, rather than to repent and believe in Jesus. The Bible's story line is said to pivot on the remaking of the world rather than on the substitutionary death of Jesus.

And in the process, Christianity becomes less about grace and faith, and more a banal religion of "Live like this, and we'll change the world." That's not Christianity; it's moralism.

A Stumbling Block and Foolishness

At the end of the day, I wonder if the impulse to shove the cross out of the center of the gospel comes from the bare fact that the world just doesn't like the cross. At best they think it is a ridiculous fairy tale, and at worst, a monstrous lie. Really, that shouldn't surprise us. Paul told us it would be the case. The message of the cross, he said, will be a stumbling block to some and foolishness to the rest!

Add to that the fact that we really *want* the world to be attracted to the gospel, and you create enormous pressure on Christians to find a way not to have to talk about "bloody cross religion" quite so much. I mean, we want the world to accept the gospel, not laugh at it, right?

But really, we should just face it. The message of the cross is going to sound like nonsense to the people around us. It's going to make us Christians sound like fools, and it most certainly is going to undermine our attempts to "relate" to non-Christians and prove to them that we're just as cool and harmless as the next guy. Christians can always get the world to think they are cool—right up to the moment they start talking about being saved by a crucified man. And that's where coolness evaporates, no matter how carefully you've cultivated it.

Even so, Scripture makes it clear that the cross *must* remain at the center of the gospel. We cannot move it to the side, and we cannot replace it with any other truth as the heart, center, and fountainhead of the good news. To do so is to present the world with something that is not saving, and that is therefore not good news at all.

The Bible actually gives us very clear instruction on how we should respond to any pressure to let the cross drift out of the center of the gospel. We are to resist it. Look at what Paul said about this in 1 Corinthians. He knew the message of the cross sounded, at best, insane to those around him. He knew they would reject the gospel because of it, that it would be a stench in their nostrils. But even in the face of that sure rejection he said, "We preach Christ crucified" (1 Cor. 1:23). In fact, he resolved to "know *nothing* among you except Jesus Christ and him cruci-fied" (1 Cor. 2:2). That's because, as he put it at the end of the book, the fact that "Christ died for our sins in accordance with the Scriptures" was not just important, and not even just *very* important. It was of "*first* importance" (1 Cor. 15:3).

And what if that brings on the ridicule of the world? What if people respond better to a gospel tilted toward the renewal of the world instead of toward the death of Christ in the place of sinners? What if people laugh at the gospel because it's about a man dying on a cross? So be it, Paul said. I'm preaching the cross. They may think it's ridiculous; they may think it's foolish. But I know "the foolishness of God is wiser than man's wisdom" (1 Cor. 1:25 NIV).

Paul made sure the cross was the central point of the gospel he preached, and we should do the same. If we let anything else become the center, we might as well be saying, "Here, let me give you a hand jumping over that wall. Trust me. You'll be fine."

8

The Power of
the Gospel

Just before I graduated from college, two of my best friends
and I decided on a whim to take a road-trip from our hometown in East Texas up to Yellowstone National Park. It was
a great trip, kind of a coming-of-age rite of passage for three
guys who were plunging headfirst into adulthood.

As you might imagine, the trip was filled with amazing
views of mountains, geysers, hot sulfur springs, and lots and
lots of moose. One morning, we all decided to spend the day
on a hike, and we all agreed that, just for kicks, we wouldn't
take a map with us. We wanted to see where the trail led.
So we packed some lunch food and our cell phones into our
backpacks and headed out.

It was a long hike, and after a while we started joking with
one another that here we were in Yellowstone National Park,
and it really didn't look much different from the woods of East
Texas where we'd all grown up. Huge pine trees surrounded
us on every side, and every once in a while we'd have to hop
over a little creek that crossed the path. But it wasn't much to
look at, really, and nerves began to fray a little.

But then, all of a sudden, before any of us really had time to notice that anything was changing, the forest cleared and we found ourselves standing at the edge of the Grand Canyon of the Yellowstone. Stretched out below us for miles was a magnificent gash in the earth. A river ran through the bottom of it, sparkling as the sun glinted off it. Birds flew below us, and low-hanging clouds sped by above, caught, I guess, in the wind currents being channeled by the canyon.

What an incredible feeling of smallness I had at that moment, staring into a dizzying expanse below me and looking into the sky. For a few moments, all three of us were—for the first time all day—speechless. And then one of my friends began to sing,

> O Lord my God, when I in awesome wonder,
> consider all the worlds thy hands have made . . .[1]

He wasn't a good singer, God bless him, but his heart was exactly right! For the next few minutes we stood at the edge of the Grand Canyon of the Yellowstone and praised the One who had created that awe-inspiring masterpiece.

Why Do We Overlook It?

You know, I think the gospel would have that same overwhelming effect on us if we took the time to stop and really think about it. How long has it been since you looked up from the earthly details of life and came face to face with the Grand Canyon of what God has done for us in the gospel—his unfathomable

---

[1] "How Great Thou Art," Stuart K. Hine, 1949; based on the poem "O Store Gud," Carl G. Boberg, 1886.

grace in forgiving people who have rebelled against him, his breathtaking plan to send his Son to suffer and die in their place, to establish the throne of the resurrected Jesus over a kingdom of perfect righteousness, and to bring those who are saved and redeemed by his blood into a new heavens and new earth where sin and evil will be forever conquered!

How is it that I let the beauty and power and vastness of that gospel be crowded out of my mind so often and for so long? Why is it that my thoughts and emotions are often dominated by silly things like whether my car is clean, or what's happening on CNN right now, or whether I was happy with my lunch today, rather than by these glorious truths? Why do I so often organize and think about my life as if I were wearing blinders, rather than in the light of eternity? Why does this gospel not permeate, all the time and all the way to the bottom, my relationships with my wife and children, my coworkers and friends and fellow church members?

I know exactly why. It's because I'm a sinner, and worldliness will continue to linger in my heart and war against me until the day Jesus comes back. But until then, I want to fight against that. I want to fight against spiritual laziness—against the drugged stupor this world constantly threatens to put me in—and I want to embrace this gospel hard and let it affect everything—my actions, affections, emotions, desires, thoughts, and will.

I hope you want that too. And I hope this small book has helped part the trees a little so you can see the grandeur of what God has done for us in Jesus. But what now? Well, let me mention just a few things—there a million others I won't mention—about how the good news of Jesus should affect our lives.

Repent and Believe

First, if you are not a Christian, thank you for reading this far in this book. I hope you've taken the opportunity to give some thought to this good news about Jesus, and I pray it has gotten deeply into your mind. For you, I think the "what now" question is actually really easy. There aren't a million things you ought to do. There is one: repent of your sins and believe in Jesus. That means recognizing your spiritual bankruptcy, acknowledging your complete inability to save yourself, and coming to Jesus as your only hope of ever being forgiven and right before God.

Becoming a Christian is not some laborious process. There's nothing to earn. Jesus has already earned everything you need. What the gospel calls you to do is to turn your heart away from sin and toward Jesus in faith—that is, trust and reliance. It calls you to come to him and say, "I know I can't save myself, Jesus, so I'm trusting you to do it for me."

And then a whole world opens up before you. But it all begins with repenting of sin and trusting in Jesus to save you.

Rest and Rejoice

If you are a Christian, then the gospel calls you first of all to rest in Jesus Christ and to rejoice in the unassailable salvation he has won for you. Because of Jesus, and because I know that I am united to him by faith, I can fight against the temptation to think that my salvation is somehow fragile or passing. Whether I feel it at any given moment, I can know—deep down beneath the swirling questions—that I belong to Jesus and that no one can snatch me out of his hand. That's because the gospel tells me that my righteous standing before God is not grounded in checking off some spiritual bingo card. Enough fruit? Check. Quiet time? Check! Spiritual conversation? Check, check, check! Great! I'm feeling *really* saved today!

How ridiculous in light of what the gospel says about Jesus! Thank God, my relationship with him is not based on my fickle will or my ability to live righteously. No, God has already pronounced his verdict over me, and it is "FORGIVEN!" Even more, that verdict will never change because it is grounded solely and forever in Jesus—his death on the cross in my place and his intercession for me even now before the throne of God.

If you are a Christian, then the cross of Jesus stands like a mountain of granite across your life, immovably testifying to God's love for you and his determination to bring you safely into his presence. It's as Paul said in Romans: "If God is for us, who can be against us? He who did not spare his own Son but gave him up for us all, how will he not also with him graciously give us all things?" (Rom. 8:31–32).

Love Christ's People

Also, Christian, the gospel should drive you to a deeper and livelier love for God's people, the church. Not one of us Christians has earned his or her way into the inheritance God has stored up for us. We are not "self-made" citizens of the kingdom. We are included in God's promises only because we know that we are dependent on Jesus Christ to save us, and we are united to him by faith.

But here's the kicker. Do you realize that the same thing is true of that brother or sister in your church who annoys you? He or she believes in and loves the same Lord Jesus that you do, and even more, he or she has been saved and forgiven by the same Lord who saved and forgave you. Think about that brother or sister you've not really taken the time to get to know because you just don't think you'd click. Think about that person with whom you have a broken relationship that you've refused to repair. Now consider that he or she loves and trusts in the same Lord you do. Consider that the same Lord who died for you, also died for him, for her.

I wonder if your understanding of the gospel of Jesus Christ—the good news that Jesus saved you even though you didn't deserve it—is deep enough to swallow up the little criticisms you have of your brothers and sisters. I wonder if it's deep enough to sink the offenses they've committed against you, even the most painful ones, and lead you to forgive them and love them just as Jesus himself has done for both of you.

I wonder if the vastness of God's love for you has increased your love for others.

Speak the Gospel to the World

Not only that, but I wonder if God's grace to you has caused you to love the world around you more, and to long to see people come to know and believe in Jesus Christ. If we truly understand the grace God has shown us, our hearts will burn to see that same grace shown to others.

After his resurrection, Jesus appeared to his disciples and told them this: "Thus it is written, that the Christ should suffer and on the third day rise from the dead, and that repentance and forgiveness of sins should be proclaimed in his name to all nations, beginning from Jerusalem." There it was, laid out in crystal clarity for the disciples—God's grand plan to save a people for himself. And then, stunningly, Jesus added this: "You are witnesses of these things" (Luke 24:46–48). I've always imagined that the color must have drained out of the disciples' faces when they heard that! God's purpose was nothing less than the redemption of the world, and here was Jesus telling them that purpose would be accomplished *through them*!

I don't know about you, but that thought makes me feel incredibly inadequate. God intends to bring about his purposes in the world through *us*? Amazing! But if you feel unworthy and inadequate, let me give you some encouragement. You *are* unworthy, and you are most certainly inadequate! How's that for encouragement? Look at us—frail, weak human beings who still struggle against sin every day of our lives. And yet Jesus says to us, "You will be my witnesses." It is through our proclaiming the gospel—whether through preaching or teaching or conversations over meals with friends, family members, and coworkers—that God has determined to save sinners.

Have you ever wondered why the angel who spoke to Cornelius in Acts 10 didn't just tell him the gospel? Why go to all the trouble of having Cornelius send for Peter, who was in an altogether different town? Really, if the angel could tell Cornelius all that, surely he could just as well have told him the gospel! But no, God has determined that the gospel will advance through the spoken words of his people—that is, through the mouths of those who have themselves embraced the good news about Jesus and have known the forgiveness that comes from him.

If you are a Christian, realize that you hold in your hands the only true message of salvation the world will ever hear. There will never be another gospel, and there is no other way for people to be saved from their sins. If your friends, family, and coworkers are ever to be saved from their sins, it will be because someone speaks the gospel of Jesus Christ to them. That's why Jesus commissions us to go into all the world, preaching and teaching this good news to the nations. It's also what Paul meant in Romans 10 when he asked, "How are they to believe in him of whom they have never heard? And how are they to hear without someone preaching?" (v. 14). There are many good things that we can do as Christians, but the fact is that most of those good things will happily be done also by people who are not Christians. But if we Christians fail to proclaim the gospel of Jesus, who else is going to do that? No one.

So let the truths of the gospel penetrate your heart and even break it for those who do not know Jesus Christ. Meditate on what it will mean for your friends, family, and coworkers to stand before God the righteous Judge apart from Jesus Christ. Remember what the grace of God has done in your own life, and imagine what he could do in theirs. Then take a deep breath, pray for God's Spirit to work, and open your mouth and speak!

Long for Him

Finally, the gospel should cause us to long for the day when our King Jesus will return to establish his kingdom fully and finally and forever. That's not a longing borne ultimately of just *being* in the kingdom; we don't long for Jesus' return just because we will live in a world where evil is conquered and justice reigns.

Those are wonderful promises, but even they are not big enough. No, if we understand the gospel rightly, we will long not so much for the kingdom as for the King. The gospel has brought us to know him and love him, and therefore to long to be with him. "I desire that they . . . may be with me where I am" Jesus said (John 17:24). And we desire to be with him, too, joining with millions of others to worship him.

The book of Revelation contains an amazing vision of what God has prepared for us who love him. It's just a hint, but you can still feel the overwhelming sense of victory, joy, rest, and finality in this picture of the redeemed worshipping Jesus Christ.

> After this I looked, and behold, a great multitude that no one could number, from every nation, from all tribes and peoples and languages, standing before the throne and before the Lamb, clothed in white robes, with palm branches in their hands, and crying out with a loud voice, "Salvation belongs to our God who sits on the throne, and to the Lamb!" (Rev. 7:9–10)

That is the day the gospel drives us to long for. Even as we slog through the trials, persecutions, irritations, temptations, distractions, apathy, and just plain weariness of this world, the gospel points us to heaven where our King Jesus—the Lamb of God who was crucified in our place and raised gloriously from the dead—now sits interceding for us. Not only so, but it calls us forward to that final day when heaven will be filled with the roaring noise of millions upon millions of forgiven voices hailing him as crucified Savior and risen King.

Special Thanks

As with any book project, with this one there are countless people to whom I owe a word of thanks. One does not learn or think in isolation, and I could spend a day just naming brothers and sisters with whom I have, for the last decade and more, been talking and thinking about the gospel. However, there are a few people to whom I want to say a special "thank you."

First, to the wonderful team at Crossway, thank you for taking a chance on an unknown author. If the Lord sees fit to use this book to edify his church, it will have been through your instrumentality.

Thanks also to the team at 9Marks for their encouragement to me to write this book, and their efforts to make it happen. Matt Schmucker's vision and passion for the health of the church around the world is inspiring, and I'm honored to know him and to work with him. Jonathan Leeman helped me tremendously in the writing of this book. Through conversations, emails, and editing, he sharpened this book. And thanks also to Bobby Jamieson, who drained untold numbers of lattes with me talking about the kingdom. What a joy it is to be on this team!

To Mark Dever, my dear brother, thank you for pushing me to write my first book. I am indebted to you in ways I'm not sure I could ever articulate. I'm proud to call you my spiritual mentor, and I am so glad our Lord surprised us both by bringing me back to Washington DC for a time. He is so kind to give us this time together.

Finally, thank you to my strong and beautiful wife, Moriah, who loves and cares for me so well, and who puts up with more than her fair share of moments when I disappear into my own head working on some knotty theological problem. I love you dearly, Babe.

Scripture Index

IX 9Marks

Building Healthy Churches

9Marks exists to equip church leaders with a biblical vision and practical resources for displaying God's glory to the nations through healthy churches.

To that end, we want to see churches characterized by these nine marks of health:

1. Expositional Preaching
2. Gospel Doctrine
3. A Biblical Understanding of Conversion and Evangelism
4. Biblical Church Membership
5. Biblical Church Discipline
6. A Biblical Concern for Discipleship and Growth
7. Biblical Church Leadership
8. A Biblical Understanding of the Practice of Prayer
9. A Biblical Understanding and Practice of Missions

Find all our Crossway titles and other resources at 9Marks.org.